PHILIPPINES

TRAVEL GUIDE 2023

A Complete Guide for Tourists on How to Explore this Vibrant Country & All Its Islands. From Manila the Capital to Palawan. What to do, Where to Stay & What to Eat.

By

Tim Hoey

PHILIPPINES TRAVEL GUIDE 2023

All right reserved. This book or any portion therefore may not be duplicated or utilized in any manner whatsoever without the express written permission of the publisher except for the use of a brief quotation in a book review.

Printed in the country or state where it is published.

@2023

CONTENTS

INTRODUCTION

CHAPTER ONE

INTRODUCTION
OVERVIEW & BRIEF HISTORY
Geographical Features & Regions
Cultural Diversity & Traditions

CHAPTER TWO

ESSENTIAL TRAVEL TIPS
VISAS & ENTRY REGULATIONS
Currency & Banking Information
Safety & Emergency Contacts
Local Customs & Etiquette

CHAPTER THREE

PLANNING YOUR TRIP
BEST TIME TO VISIT
Transportation Options Within

PHILIPPINES TRAVEL GUIDE 2023

Accommodation Options
Packing Tips & Essentials

CHAPTER FOUR

MANILA: THE CAPITAL
EXPLORING THE CITY`S HISTORIC SITES
Iconic Landmark & Attractions
Culinary Delights & Local Cuisine
Shopping & Entertainment Options

CHAPTER FIVE

ISLAND HOPPING
Popular Island Destinations & Their Unique Features
Beaches, Snorkeling, & Diving Spots
Island Hopping Itineraries & Activities

CHAPTER SIX

ADVENTURE & NATURE
HIKING & TREKKING TRAILS
Volcanos Exploration
Waterfalls & Natural Wonders
Wildlife & Marine Sanctuaries

CHAPTER SEVEN

LOCAL CUISINE & DINING
POPULAR FILIPINO DISHES & STREET FOOD
Regional Specialties & Flavors
Dining Etiquette & Food Markets

CHAPTER EIGHT

HISTORICAL & HERITAGE SITES
UNESCO WORLD HERITAGE SITES
Museums & Historical Landmarks
Spanish Colonial Architecture

CHAPTER NINE

CULTURAL IMMERSION
INDIGENOUS TRIBES & CULTURAL EXPERIENCES
Festivals & Celebrations
Homestays & Community Based-Tourism

CHAPTER TEN

PRACTICAL TRAVEL TIPS
LOCAL TRANSPORTATION TIPS
Health & Safety Precautions

PHILIPPINES TRAVEL GUIDE 2023

Sustainable Travel Practices

CONCLUSION

INTRODUCTION

An exhilarating feeling of anticipation rushed through my veins as the jet touched down in Manila in the early morning gloom. I was about to set out on a journey that would alter the path of my life forever. It was my first trip to the enthralling Philippine archipelago, which would later serve as my inspiration and serve as the basis for this travel manual.

My feet landed on the warm, sandy sands of Boracay, and I immediately realized I had found a secret paradise. I was enticed to continue exploring by the turquoise waters lapping delicately against the snow-white beaches. I moved through the streets of the Philippines, taking in the warm smiles of the people and the enticing aromas of street food cooking on every corner.

The incredible variety of vistas as I traveled the archipelago astounded me. The limestone cliffs of El Nido towered magnificently over the crystal-clear seas below, while the emerald rice terraces of Banaue appeared to defy gravity. As I saw the flaming tones of a sunset surround the Chocolate Hills of Bohol and the rhythmic dance of fireflies illuminating the romantic riverbanks of Puerto Princesa, my heart overflowed with awe.

The sincere kindness and unwavering attitude of the Filipino people left an enduring impression on my soul above and beyond the breathtaking environment. Their contagious happiness and tenacity served as examples of the power of the human spirit.

my life-changing experience served as my inspiration for my travel guidebook, which attempts to convey the essence of the Philippines. I want to encourage other travelers to create their own amazing experiences in this place of unending beauty by sharing the secret spots, unwritten tales, and insider knowledge that I have learned along the journey.

Join me as we explore the Philippines' treasures, a country where dreams come true and where every step unveils a new chapter in the incredible story of a land unlike any other.

CHAPTER ONE

Introduction

Overview & Brief History

In Southeast Asia, the 7,641-island archipelago known as the Philippines is a riveting travel destination that presents a rich tapestry of historical significance, cultural diversity, and unmatched natural beauty. The geography, population, languages, and religions of the nation are briefly covered in the first section of this guidebook before moving on to a succinct examination of its fascinating history.

Demographics and Geography

The South China Sea and the Philippine Sea surround the Philippines, which is located in the western Pacific Ocean. The nation is renowned for its breathtaking scenery, which includes verdant mountains, terraced rice fields, and clean beaches with azure oceans. Despite being vulnerable to typhoons and earthquakes due to its strategic placement in the Pacific Ring of Fire, the country is blessed with stunning natural treasures.

PHILIPPINES TRAVEL GUIDE 2023

The Philippines, which has a population of nearly 110 million, is a multicultural and diversified nation. Although the vast majority of Filipinos are of Malay heritage, the nation has historically been shaped by many other civilizations. More than 170 languages and dialects are spoken throughout the archipelago in addition to the official languages of English and Filipino.

Culture and Religion: The Philippines is renowned for its deeply ingrained religious customs. Roman Catholicism is the most popular religion in the Philippines, where the majority of people identify as Christians. This legacy can be linked to the Spanish colonial era, which had a big impact on the nation's festivals, culture, and architecture.

Additionally, the Philippines have a rich and varied cultural legacy. Woodcarving, weaving, and ceramics are a few examples of traditional arts and crafts that are valued and conserved. Festivals like Sinulog, Ati-Atihan, and Panagbenga highlight the nation's vivacious spirit by fusing native traditions with Christian ones.

Short History

The history of the Philippines is a fascinating story of pre-colonial cultures, colonial control, and freedom movements. The archipelago has been populated since ancient times, and early human sites can be found dating back 67,000 years. The Austronesian peoples who first inhabited the area established the groundwork for the rich cultural heritage of the Filipino people.

The entrance of the Spanish in the 16th century signaled a turning point in Philippine history. The first European settlement in Cebu was established in 1521 by Spanish explorers under the command of Ferdinand Magellan. The local people were progressively brought under the rule and influence of the Spanish during the following few decades as they established Manila as the nation's capital and converted them to Catholicism.

The Philippines were molded by over three centuries of Spanish domination, which forever altered its religion, language, and culture. However, the Philippine Revolution of 1896 was ultimately brought about by a growing demand for independence. The nation proclaimed its independence from Spain on June 12, 1898, only to later cede its independence to the United States as a result of the Treaty of Paris.

The Philippines did not become fully independent from American rule until 1946 when it did so and became Asia's first democratic republic. In contrast, the nation endured many difficulties in the decades that followed, including World War II and the martial law regime of President Ferdinand Marcos. The EDSA Revolution, a nonviolent popular revolt in 1986, brought democracy back to the Philippines and opened a new chapter in its history.

Since then, the Philippines has gone through phases of economic expansion, governmental changes, and ongoing social issue-solving initiatives. The nation is now recognized as a thriving and resilient one that embraces its rich history while looking to the future with optimism.

The Philippines is an alluring location with a lengthy, rich history. The nation offers a blend of natural beauty, great hospitality, and a distinctive cultural identity thanks to its diversified topography and cosmopolitan society. Exploring the Philippines is like traveling through time and learning about the rich customs and tales that have defined this alluring archipelago.

Geographical Features & Regions

This tropical haven Philippines is home to a wide variety of geographical features, including towering mountains, lush rainforests, and coral reefs in addition to immaculate beaches. We shall examine the main geographical regions of the Philippines in this section, each having distinctive traits and attractions.

The largest and most populous island in the Philippines is called Luzon, and it is situated in the northernmost region of the archipelago. Manila, the nation's capital, as well as breathtaking landscapes and cultural treasures, may be found there. The gorgeous Cordillera mountain range, famous for its Banaue rice terraces and the bustling city of Baguio, a well-liked summer getaway, is located in the northern portion of Luzon. As the "Rice Bowl of the Philippines," the central region of Luzon is home to the huge and productive Central Luzon Plain. The Bicol Peninsula, known for its majestic Mayon Volcano and scenic beaches, dominates the southern section of Luzon.

The Visayas region, which is in the center of the Philippine archipelago, is made up of a number of significant islands, including Cebu, Bohol, and Negros. Divers and beach lovers will find this area to be a refuge because of its immaculate white-sand beaches, clear waters, and abundant marine life. The Visayas provide cultural treasures in addition to their natural beauty, like the historic city of Cebu with its Spanish colonial architecture and the renowned Chocolate Hills in Bohol.

The second-largest island in the Philippines is called Mindanao, and it is located in the country's southern region. It is well-known for its various indigenous cultures, beautiful scenery, and abundant biodiversity. Mount Apo, the Philippines' tallest mountain, as well as breathtaking waterfalls like Tinuy-an Falls and Aliwagwag Falls, may be found in Mindanao. Also available in the area are chances for adventure travel, such as white-water rafting in Cagayan de Oro and surfing in Siargao, known as the "Surfing Capital of the Philippines."

The province of Palawan, which includes the main island of Palawan and the smaller outlying islands, is situated in the western portion of the Philippines. Due to its breathtaking vistas and abundant marine species, it is routinely rated as one of the best islands in the world. There are several UNESCO World Heritage Sites in Palawan, including the Tubbataha Reefs Natural Park and the Puerto Princesa Subterranean River National Park. Popular vacation spots El Nido and Coron include stunning limestone cliffs, clean beaches, and clear waters.

Another fascinating island in the Philippines is Mindoro, which is situated southwest of Luzon. The island, which is divided between the provinces of Oriental Mindoro and Occidental Mindoro, provides a variety of cultural and natural attractions. Puerto Galera, a popular diving and snorkeling location, is found in Mindoro's northern region. On the other hand, the southern region is home to the Mangyan indigenous villages, which exhibit their distinctive customs and crafts, and Mount Halcon, one of the Philippines' most difficult mountains to climb.

Travelers can experience a wide range of activities in the Philippines thanks to its diverse regions and geographical features, from hiking through beautiful mountains to seeing the country's rich cultures. The Philippines is a magnificent location that appeals to a variety of interests thanks to the contributions of Luzon, Visayas, Mindanao, Palawan, and Mindoro, each of which adds its own special attractions. In order to help guests get started on their journey to this gorgeous archipelago, this section gives a general overview of these areas.

Cultural Diversity & Traditions

The Philippines is a nation famous for its vibrant customs and rich cultural variety. The archipelago has a mingling of influences from indigenous populations, Spanish invaders, Chinese traders, and American occupiers. It has about 7,000 islands, each inhabited by a different ethnic group. The fascinating cultural diversity of the Philippines is highlighted in this section, which also examines its enduring traditions and practices.

Indigenous Communities: The Philippines is home to a large number of indigenous communities, each with its own cultural history. From the T'boli in Mindanao to the Igorots in the mountainous areas of Luzon, these peoples exhibit their traditions through vibrant festivals, exquisite handicrafts, and age-old rituals. Visitors can become fully immersed in the tribal way of life by taking part in traditional dances, sampling regional cuisine, and admiring the skillful weaving of fabrics and hand-carving of items.

Spanish Influences: The Philippines' culture bears the unmistakable imprint of centuries of Spanish colonial rule. Catholicism was brought by the Spanish, who established it as the main religion. Catholicism's impact is visible in the vast number of churches and religious celebrations held throughout the nation. The great Sinulog Festival in Cebu, which celebrates the devotion to the Santo Nio (Child Jesus), and the Pahiyas Festival in Lucban, where houses are decorated with vibrant rice decorations as thanksgiving gifts, are notable occasions.

Chinese Influences: The Chinese, particularly in trade and cuisine, have greatly influenced Philippine culture. Long before the Spanish came, Chinese traders left an enduring impact. The world's oldest Chinatown, located in Manila's Binondo neighborhood, is proof of this intercultural interchange. Visitors can stroll through its busy streets, go to Taoist temples, and savor real Chinese food like dim sum and noodles.

American Influence: The Philippines' nearly five decades of American control have left a profound mark on the country's cultural environment. English became widely spoken, and various facets of culture were influenced by the West. In addition to observing American festivals like Halloween and Valentine's Day, Filipinos also adopted American pastimes like basketball. With the emergence of Filipino pop, rock, and hip-hop, the blending of American and Filipino culture is also audible in the thriving music industry.

Festivals & Celebrations: The Philippines is renowned for its vibrant and exuberant festivals that honor historical, religious, and cultural occasions. In order to celebrate the Santo Nio, participants in one of the most well-known events, the Ati-Atihan in Kalibo, Aklan, dress in traditional Visayan garb and apply black soot to their faces. Other noteworthy events are the Panagbenga Festival in Baguio City, which has a spectacular floral parade, and the Kadayawan Festival in Davao City, which honors the indigenous roots of the city.

Gastronomy and cuisine: The flavors of Filipino food are a delicious combination of those from many civilizations. Filipino cuisine appeals to a wide range of palates, from the acidic and savory flavor of adobo to the sour broth of sinigang. Every region has a signature food, such as the fiery cuisine of Bicol and the Lechon (roasted pig) of Cebu. Traditional Arts & Crafts: Filipinos have a long history of producing fine handicrafts, so exploring local markets and food stands is a great opportunity to experience the Philippines' culinary diversity. Filipino artistry displays the nation's cultural past in everything from beautiful woodcarvings and pottery to hand-woven textiles like the pia and jusi. In locations like the Ilocos region, well-known for its weaving traditions, or the towns of Paete and Angono, well-known for their woodcarving and painting traditions, respectively, visitors can observe experienced artisans at work.

Travelers seeking an immersive experience will find the Philippines to be an interesting location due to its cultural diversity and traditions. Visitors will gain a deeper understanding of the Philippines' remarkable legacy by investigating the indigenous cultures, Spanish and American influences, Chinese ties, American influence, vibrant festivals, delectable cuisine, and traditional arts and crafts of the nation. Visitors may genuinely appreciate the friendliness and politeness of the people while making lifelong memories of their voyage through the archipelago by embracing the country's cultural diversity.

CHAPTER TWO

Essential Travel Tips

Visas & Entry Regulations

It is crucial to comprehend the visa requirements and entrance restrictions in order to secure a simple and hassle-free entry into the Philippines, which has grown to be a popular vacation spot for travelers from around the world. We will give you all the information you need to organize your trip to the Philippines in this section.

Visa Exemptions: For travel and commerce, the Philippine government grants visa exemptions to nationals of a number of other nations. Visitors can enter the nation without a visa and remain there for a set amount of time thanks to these exemptions. Currently, citizens of the United States, Canada, the United Kingdom, Australia, New Zealand, most of the European Union countries, and numerous more nations can enter the Philippines without a visa for up to 30 days. It's important to remember that these visa exemptions could change, so it's always a good idea to double-check with the Philippine embassy or consulate in your area before your trip.

Visa on Arrival: The Philippines also has a visa-on-arrival program for those who do not qualify for visa exemptions. This makes it possible for travelers to the nation to obtain a visa at a few of the nation's international airports and seaports. The duration of the visa on arrival is up to 59 days, and an extra 29 days may be added. But it's imperative to make sure your passport is valid for at least six months past the length of time you plan to spend there and that you have a return or onward ticket.

Pre-Entry Visa: You must apply for a pre-entry visa at a Philippine embassy or consulate in your home country if you want to stay in the Philippines for a period of time longer than the visa-free or visa-on-arrival term. Depending on the reason for your travel, there are many pre-entry visas available, including tourist, business, student, and work visas. Consult the embassy or consulate in advance to learn more about the requirements and processing periods.

Extension of Stay: You may request an extension at a Bureau of Immigration (BI) office in the Philippines if you are already there and want to stay longer than is legally allowed. Extensions are frequently granted for up to 59 days, but they have to be asked for before your existing visa expires. It is crucial to follow the immigration requirements because overstaying your visa might result in fines and other consequences.

Special permissions and Clearances: Travelers must get special permissions or clearances before visiting various regions of the Philippines, including the Autonomous Region in Muslim Mindanao (ARMM) and some sections of Palawan. These licenses are usually needed for security or environmental conservation concerns and are obtained from the proper governmental organizations or municipal authorities. It is advised to inquire about any particular permits necessary for your desired destinations with the Philippine Department of Tourism or the local tourism office.

For a hassle-free trip to the Philippines, it is essential to comprehend the visa requirements and entry laws. Regardless of whether you qualify for visa exemptions, require an on-site visa, or need to apply for a pre-entry visa, it is imperative that you plan your trip appropriately, make sure you have the required paperwork, and check that your passports are still valid. In order to have a smooth and comfortable stay in the stunning islands of the Philippines, keep in mind to check for any updates or changes to the visa laws before your departure and to always abide by immigration regulations.

Currency & Banking Information

Learning about the local currency and banking system is crucial while making travel plans to the Philippines. This section will arm you with crucial knowledge for navigating the Philippine financial system, guaranteeing a simple and straightforward financial experience while traveling.

The Philippine Peso (PHP) is the country of the Philippines' official currency. It is split into centavos and represented by the symbol "₱". Banknotes come in denominations of 20, 50, 100, 200, 500, and 1,000 pesos; coins come in 1, 5, 10, and 25 pesos and 1, 5, and 10 centavo denominations. For everyday transactions, it's advised to carry a variety of smaller denomination bills and coins, as it could be difficult to receive change for larger bills in some locations.

Exchange rates: In every region of the nation, banks and hotels that are allowed to exchange foreign currency are available. While exchange rates may slightly vary depending on the area, banks frequently provide reasonable rates. Before making any currency conversion, it is wise to examine rates to make sure you are getting the best deal possible. The majority of significant airports, shopping centers, and tourist destinations include currency exchange facilities.

Banking Services: The Philippines has a well-established banking system with a sizable network of domestic and foreign banks. The following are some crucial details concerning the nation's banking services to be aware of:

- a) Banks: The biggest regional banks in the Philippines are the Philippine National Bank (PNB), Metropolitan Bank and Trust Company (Metrobank), Bank of the Philippine Islands (BPI), Banco de Oro (BDO), and Bank of the Philippine Islands (BPI). These financial institutions have locations all around the nation and offer a variety of services like currency exchange, ATM withdrawals, and international money transfers.
- b) ATMs: There are many automated teller machines (ATMs) in big cities and well-traveled regions. Visa, Mastercard, and American Express are a few of the widely used foreign debit and credit cards that are accepted. Cash can be easily withdrawn in the local currency via ATMs. For increased security, it is advised to use ATMs found inside bank buildings.
- c) Credit Cards: In urban locations, hotels, upscale eateries, and sizable retail stores all take credit cards. Visa and Mastercard are the two credit cards that are used the most, followed by American Express and Diners Club. To prevent any potential problems with card transactions, it is advisable to let your credit card company know about your vacation intentions.

d) Traveler's Checks: Although they were formerly a common choice, traveler's checks have been less common in recent years. It might be difficult to locate banks that still take traveler's checks, and many establishments have stopped accepting them. It is advised to use cash, debit, or credit cards for your purchases.

Security and Safety: Just as in any other trip destination, it's crucial to take security measures to protect your money and financial transactions. Observe the following advice:

a) Use ATMs in well-lit, secure areas, ideally inside bank buildings.
b) Be discreet with your PIN number and hide the keyboard when entering it.
c) Be aware of your surroundings and refrain from flashing big amounts of cash in front of others.
d) If your credit or debit cards are lost or stolen, notify your bank right away.
e) Think about keeping some cash on you in case of emergencies or places where cards might not be accepted.

For a smooth travel experience, it is crucial to comprehend the Philippine currency and financial system. Learn about accessible banking services, exchange rates, and local currencies. You can protect your funds while taking advantage of the stunning views and activities the Philippines has to offer with careful planning and measures.

Safety & Emergency Contacts

It's crucial to put your safety first when visiting the stunning Philippine archipelago. Despite the country's beautiful scenery and welcoming people, it's important to be aware of any threats and take the appropriate safety measures. This section offers important safety advice and emergency contacts to provide a worry-free and secure trip throughout the Philippines.

Safety Advice:

Stay Up to Date: Investigate the current state of safety in the particular areas you plan to visit before your trip. Keep abreast of any travel warnings issued by the embassy or consulate of your nation and heed their advice.

Getting comprehensive travel insurance that covers medical emergencies, trip cancellations, and personal possessions is highly advised. If you intend to participate in hobbies like diving or hiking, make sure your policy covers them.

Personal Property: Always keep your valuables secure, including passports, money, and devices. When hotel safes are available, use them. You might also want to carry a safe bag or a money belt to ward off pickpockets.

Transportation: When using public transportation, pick respected drivers and stay away from nighttime solo trips, particularly in outlying locations. If you intend to rent a car, make sure the agency is reputable and make a note of the emergency contact information offered by the rental firm.

Be Alert: Keep a close eye on your surroundings, particularly in crowded locations or tourist hotspots where thieves may be active. Displaying pricey jewelry or significant sums of money should be avoided as they may draw unwelcome attention.

Water and Street cuisine: The Philippines is renowned for its delectable street cuisine, but use caution when consuming it. To lower your chance of contracting a foodborne disease, choose stalls with a high volume of customers and where the food is freshly prepared. To avoid ingesting tainted water, drink bottled water or use a water filter.

Natural disasters such as typhoons, earthquakes, and volcanic eruptions are common in the Philippines. Follow any warnings or recommendations for an evacuation made by local authorities and keep an eye on weather forecasts. Evacuation routes should be known to you, and a plan should be in place.

Respect Local Customs: Become acquainted with the regional traditions and customs before traveling there. To prevent any potential disputes or misunderstandings, respect religious sites, dress modestly where necessary, and abide by local customs.

Emergency Contacts: When traveling in the Philippines, it's crucial to have access to vital emergency contacts. Here are some crucial numbers you ought to remember:

- a) Police: Dial 911 or 117 (the Philippine National Police hotline) in the event of an emergency or if you need police help.
- b) Call 911 or 112 (Emergency Medical Services) in case of an ambulance or medical emergency. Keep the information for your travel insurance close at hand.
- c) Fire: Call 911 or 117 (Bureau of Fire Protection) in the event of a fire or a fire-related emergency.
- d) Coast Guard: Dial 911 or (02) 8527-8487 to reach the Philippine Coast Guard in cases of maritime emergencies or concerns.
- e) Tourism Department maintains a hotline for travelers that is available 24/7. Contact information for them includes (02) 8527-0990 and dot.officeofproductresearch@gmail.com.
- f) Embassy or Consulate: Keep the details for the embassy or consulate of your nation in the Philippines. In the event of an emergency, misplaced passports, or other urgent circumstances, they can offer aid.

In case of a dead battery or poor service, don't forget to program these emergency numbers into your phone and keep a hard copy on hand. Find out where the closest pharmacies, medical facilities, and hospitals are in the places you intend to visit.

You can travel safely and worry-free across the many fascinating places in the Philippines by heeding this safety advice and having your emergency contacts close at hand. Your safety is our top priority, so you may completely enjoy the nation's breathtaking scenery, lively culture, and kind people.

Local Customs & Etiquette

To ensure a comfortable and polite visit to the Philippines, it is imperative to become familiar with the regional customs and etiquette. Understanding and respecting the cultural standards of the Filipino people would make it easier for you to go around the nation. Filipinos are recognized for their warm hospitality and welcoming demeanor. Following are some crucial customs and etiquette rules to remember:

Respect and greetings: Being respectful and courteous is very important to Filipinos. To honor elders or those in positions of power, it is common to use the phrases "po" and "opo" while addressing someone. The traditional greeting is a handshake, but you should also expect hugs and cheek kisses, especially from close friends and relatives.

Personal Space: People frequently stand or sit near one another in the Philippines because Filipinos are generally at ease in close quarters. Always respect personal space and be considerate of others' comfort levels, though. If unsure, take advice from the locals in your vicinity.

Dining Etiquette: Filipinos take their food very seriously, and meals are frequently shared with others. It is traditional to hold off on starting to eat until the host or the oldest person has done so. It's polite to accept second helpings when dining at someone's house as a token of gratitude. It is considered disrespectful to point with cutlery, therefore refrain from doing so. Instead, use your right hand, or if required, a serving spoon.

Shoes and Footwear: It is traditional to take off your shoes or sandals before entering someone's home. Particularly while traveling to religious locations or rural areas, this practice keeps the flooring clean. Watch out for a stack of shoes near the entryway or take the locals' lead.

Respect for Elders: There is a significant tradition of elder respect in the Philippines. The terms "Kuya" for older brothers or male friends and "Ate" for older sisters or female friends are used to refer to older persons.

Utilizing these titles demonstrates deference and fosters a cordial relationship.

Modest Dress: The majority of Filipinos dress modestly, especially in rural regions and at religious locations. It is advisable to wear modestly, covering your shoulders and knees, when visiting places of worship or going to formal occasions. Although more casual wear is permissible on beaches and in resorts, it is still essential to respect local traditions and stay away from overtly provocative attire.

Filipinos have a long history of being kind and offering gifts. It is normal to provide a small present when you go to someone's house, such as food, flowers, or candy. To show respect, it's crucial to give the gift with both hands. Similar to this, when receiving a present, accept it politely with both hands and show your gratitude.

Politeness with "Pasalubong": "Pasalubong" is the custom of bringing presents or souvenirs for loved ones after a vacation. Bringing pasalubong for loved ones is considered considerate and polite, especially if they have requested it. This kind of deed is valued highly and is considered a means of exchanging knowledge and demonstrating concern.

English is a commonly used and understood language in the Philippines, especially in urban areas. To demonstrate respect for the community, nevertheless, understanding a few fundamental Filipino expressions like "Salamat" (Welcome) and "Mabuhay" (Thank you) can go a long way. A few words in Filipino are frequently welcomed with enthusiasm and friendly response.

You will not only demonstrate respect for Filipino culture by following these etiquette and customs rules, but you will also improve your trip experience. As a result of the locals' increased willingness to help and interact with you and their appreciation for your efforts, you'll have enduring recollections of your time in the stunning Philippines.

PHILIPPINES TRAVEL GUIDE 2023

CHAPTER THREE

Planning Your Trip

Best Time to Visit

The Philippines has a wide variety of attractions to suit all kinds of visitors. The archipelago offers something for everyone, from beautiful beaches and verdant mountains to bustling festivals and cultural heritage sites. The optimum time to visit the Philippines, however, may substantially improve your experience and guarantee that you get the most out of your vacation. This section will look at the numerous things to think about when organizing your trip to this fascinating nation.

Climatic patterns

The dry season and the wet season are two different seasons that define the Philippine climate. The wet season normally lasts from May to October, and the dry season typically lasts from November to April. It's vital to remember that because of the country's geographic diversity, weather patterns can fluctuate between different places.

PHILIPPINES TRAVEL GUIDE 2023

(November to April) Dry Season:

Most people agree that the greatest time to visit the Philippines is during the dry season. This time of year is perfect for beach activities, island hopping, and exploring outdoor sites because the weather is typically sunny and comfortable. Divers particularly enjoy this time of year because of the calm waters, which offer great visibility and a wealth of marine life. Major celebrations like the Ati-Atihan in Kalibo and the Sinulog in Cebu also take place in the dry season, providing a rare chance to see lively cultural festivities.

(May to October) Wet Season:

The rainy season has its own beauty and benefits, even though it occasionally brings rain and higher humidity. During this time, waterfalls are at their most magnificent and the landscapes turn lush green. The wet season is also regarded as the off-peak travel period, so you'll see fewer tourists and have a higher chance of finding cheap lodging. The wet season can be a great option if you don't mind the occasional downpour and want a more affordable vacation. But it's important to monitor weather reports and be ready for potential delays in outdoor activities.

Considerations for Regions

Because of the Philippines' varied topography, the weather can differ greatly from one place to another.

When making travel plans, it's crucial to take the local climate into account.

Region of Northern Luzon and the Cordillera:

Due to their higher height, the northern half of Luzon and the Cordillera region have colder temperatures. The beautiful rice terraces, attractive scenery, and distinctive cultural history of these regions are well renowned. The dry season is the ideal time to travel because the cooler temperatures and clear skies enhance outdoor exploring.

Visayas and Palawan: The weather in the Visayas region, which is home to well-known vacation spots like Cebu, Bohol, and Boracay, is generally stable throughout the year. Planning your trip during the dry season, which lasts from November to April, is advised because the rainy season might occasionally bring typhoons. Similar weather patterns apply to Palawan, which is known for its gorgeous beaches and picturesque surroundings. The perfect time to visit is when it's time for the dry season.

Mindanao: Compared to other areas, Mindanao, the southernmost major island in the Philippines, has a peculiar weather pattern. Even though there is still a dry season from November to April, it is less severe and rainfall is spread out more evenly throughout the year. To prevent potential interruptions brought on by severe rains, it is advised to schedule your visit during the dry season.

The ideal time to travel to the Philippines relies on a number of variables, including preferred weather, geographic considerations, and chosen activities. The dry season, which lasts from November to April, is typically advised due to its bright and comfortable weather, while the rainy season, which lasts from May to October, has the advantage of fewer tourists and cheaper lodging. The Philippines will unquestionably enchant you with its natural beauty, gracious hospitality, and vibrant culture, regardless of the season.

Transportation Options Within

Since the Philippines is an archipelago with more than 7,000 islands, getting throughout the nation requires transportation. The Philippines provides a variety of transportation choices to meet the demands of any traveler, from crowded metropolis to far-flung beach locations. This section will examine the many transportation options available throughout the nation, enabling you to travel around its varied topography and take in its vivacious culture.

Flights: The fastest way to travel over great distances between the Philippines' largest islands is by air. There are numerous domestic airlines in the nation that run daily flights between popular tourist locations and major cities. Manila's Ninoy Aquino International Airport (NAIA), which also acts as a hub for domestic flights, is the city's primary international entry point. Mactan-Cebu International Airport, Clark International Airport, and Davao International Airport are a few additional significant airports. To get the best deals and guarantee availability during the busiest travel times, it is advised to book domestic flights in advance.

Buses: Within the Philippines, buses are a common means of transportation for both short and long distances. They provide an affordable means of getting between cities and towns. There are numerous bus companies that run routes around the nation, with air-conditioned buses being the most popular choice for longer distances. There are established bus terminals in major cities including Manila, Cebu, and Davao, although itineraries can change depending on the location. It is advised to purchase tickets in advance, particularly on holidays and weekends.

Jeepneys: In the Philippines, jeepneys are a recognizable form of transportation. These vibrant cars, which were originally converted from American military jeeps after World War II, have come to represent Filipino culture. Within cities and towns, jeepneys run following predetermined routes as shared taxis. They offer an affordable method to commute locally and experience short-distance travel. Even while jeepneys can be packed, they provide a distinctive cultural experience and a chance to meet people. A conductor normally passes through the van during the voyage to collect the fare.

Tricycles: In the Philippines, especially in smaller towns and rural regions, tricycles are a common method of transportation. These three-wheeled motorized vehicles are made up of a motorcycle and a sidecar that can hold two to three people. Depending on the area, tricycles can be rented privately or used for public transportation. Since tricycles frequently don't have set pricing, haggling over fares is typical. They are a practical choice for quick journeys within a town or to get to places that are difficult for bigger cars to reach.

Due to the nation's large number of islands, ferries, and boats are essential for inter-island travel. Many ferries run regular services between significant ports, providing both passenger and vehicular transportation. For instance, from Manila, you can take a ferry to well-known locations like Boracay, Palawan, or Bohol. Smaller vessels called bangkas or pump boats are also available for travel to distant islands and quiet beaches. Checking departure hours in advance is advised because these smaller vessels could not operate on a set schedule.

Trains: The Philippines' train network is slowly growing, although not being as comprehensive as some other nations' networks. The Philippine National Railways (PNR), the nation's primary rail system, links

Metro Manila to neighboring provinces like Bulacan and Laguna. Additionally, cities with light rail systems, like Manila and Cebu, provide a practical alternative to get around the city's traffic. Trains are a great way to avoid clogged roads, especially during rush hour.

Ridesharing and Taxis:

In big cities, taxis are frequently available, while ride-sharing services like Grab are also well-liked. Taxis are typically metered, but it's crucial to make sure the meter is on or to agree on a charge before the trip begins. Ride-sharing services enable you to reserve a car through a smartphone app and offer a practical and frequently less expensive alternative. Taxis and ride-sharing services are both helpful for moving about cities, particularly when carrying luggage or at odd hours.

Always make transportation arrangements in advance, especially for long-distance trips and at busy times of the year. When selecting a mode of transportation, keep in mind the cost, convenience, and trip time. Accept local forms of transportation to fully experience the distinctive culture of the Philippines and meet its warm inhabitants. Enjoy the tour as you discover this tropical paradise's breathtaking vistas and energetic cities.

Accommodation Options

PHILIPPINES TRAVEL GUIDE 2023

To have a comfortable and enjoyable journey while touring the stunning Philippine archipelago, it is crucial to locate the ideal lodging. There are numerous possibilities, from opulent resorts to inexpensive guesthouses, so there is something to fit every traveler's preferences and price range. This section will examine the various lodging possibilities and offer suggestions for various locations across the nation.

Luxury Hotels and Resorts:

The Philippines is home to numerous opulent resorts and hotels that provide first-rate amenities and top-notch service. Popular locations like Boracay, Palawan, and Cebu offer great options whether you're searching for a coastal paradise or a mountain hideaway. These accommodations provide large rooms, private balconies, swimming pools, spa services, and fine dining options. Amanpulo Resort in Palawan, Shangri-La's Boracay Resort and Spa, and the Farm at San Benito in Batangas are a few well-known examples of luxury resorts.

Mid-Range Hotels and Boutique Accommodations: Mid-Range Hotels and Boutique Accommodations are fantastic options for tourists looking for comfort and economy. These businesses strike a mix between value and quality, frequently offering cozy lodgings, practical locations, and welcoming staff. In locations like Manila, Cebu City, and Davao City, where you'll discover a variety of options to meet your needs, look for well-reviewed hotels. Additionally, in places like Vigan, Baguio, or Dumaguete, boutique lodging options like bed & breakfasts or heritage houses can offer a distinctive and tailored experience.

Homestays and guesthouses:

Guesthouses and homestays are excellent alternatives for travelers on a tight budget or who want to fully experience the local way of life. These lodgings frequently provide reasonable pricing, a welcoming atmosphere, and chances to interact with local hosts. You can discover guesthouses and homestays in well-known backpacker locations like El Nido, Siargao, and Banaue that provide modest amenities, shared facilities, and an opportunity to meet other visitors. They are ideal for travelers to the Philippines who seek community and authenticity.

Vacation rentals and Airbnb units are options to explore if you want a more independent and at-home feel. You can discover a property that meets your needs among the wide range of apartments, villas, and houses offered for short-term stays. Given that it frequently offers additional space, cooking amenities, and the chance to experience local life, this choice is especially helpful for families or larger groups traveling together. A variety of vacation rental alternatives are available in well-known locations including Tagaytay, Baguio, and Batanes, all of which have breathtaking vistas and distinctive experiences.

Eco-lodges & nature retreats: The Philippines is endowed with extraordinary natural beauty, and these establishments let you experience it while having the least possible influence on the environment. These lodgings frequently offer a tranquil getaway and access to outdoor pursuits like hiking, snorkeling, or bird-watching because they are situated in inaccessible or environmentally sensitive places. Eco-lodges include places like Dedon Island Resort in Siargao, Nurture Wellness Village in Tagaytay, and Danjugan Island Eco Resort in Negros Occidental.

To guarantee your chosen choice, remember to reserve your accommodations far in advance, especially during busy travel times. Always check internet reviews, compare pricing, and take the location's proximity to your planned activities into consideration.

The Philippines has a variety of lodging choices to suit different tastes and budgets. Everywhere in the nation, you may discover accommodations that meet your needs, whether you're looking for luxury, affordability, cultural immersion, or a natural getaway. You may improve your trip experience and make enduring memories in this tropical paradise by carefully selecting the proper lodging.

Packing Tips & Essentials

A trip to the stunning Philippine archipelago can be made more enjoyable by deliberately and efficiently packing for it. When choosing your travel necessities, take into account the tropical climate, varied scenery, and colorful culture. To help you get ready for your wonderful experience in the Philippines, we'll provide you with some important packing advice in this section.

Lightweight, breathable attire:

The Philippines is renowned for having warm, muggy weather all year long. Pack breathable materials like cotton or linen that are lightweight and loose-fitting. Choose comfortable clothing like shorts, T-shirts, sundresses, and skirts to keep you cool. When traveling to mountainous areas or during cooler evenings, don't forget to bring a lightweight sweater or jacket.

Swimwear & Beach Essentials: The Philippines, home to more than 7,000 islands, is renowned for its magnificent beaches and pristine waters. Don't forget to bring a beach towel, a cover-up for the beach, and your favorite swimsuit. For sun protection and hydration on your beach outings, you also need sunscreen, sunglasses, a hat, and a reusable water bottle.

Footwear: It's crucial to pack appropriate footwear due to the Philippines' varied terrain. In cities and when exploring them, a pair of supportive walking shoes or sneakers will come in handy. Pack sturdy hiking sandals or waterproof shoes if you intend to hike or explore a rural region. Sandals and flip-flops are ideal for informal outings and trips to the beach.

Defending against the elements:

Prepare for the weather in the Philippines so you can enjoy it to the fullest. When traveling during the rainy season (June to November), you must bring a lightweight raincoat or poncho. Don't forget to bring bug spray to keep off mosquitoes and other insects, especially if you intend to travel through wooded areas.

Electronics & Travel Adapters: The Philippines utilizes Type A, B, and C electrical outlets; therefore, you must pack a universal travel adapter to power your electronics. Pack a camera or a smartphone with a high-quality camera if you want to document the breathtaking landscapes and the colorful cultures you encounter. To keep your devices charged, don't forget to include extra batteries, memory cards, and a power bank.

essential records

Never leave the house without your essential travel documents. Make sure your passport is current and has at least six months left on it. Additionally, it's a good idea to bring a photocopy of your passport, information about your trip insurance, and any required visas. Keep these papers in a safe location, like a money belt or a water-resistant travel pouch.

A first aid kit including medications:

Make sure to carry enough prescription medication for the duration of your vacation if you need to take any. A modest first aid bag including necessary supplies like bandages, antiseptic cream, pain medicines, and any personal drugs you might require is also a good idea. Before leaving for the Philippines, discuss any necessary immunizations with your healthcare physician.

Travel essentials and money:

Carry a combination of cards and cash because, especially in remote locations, some businesses might not accept credit cards or may only have restricted access to ATMs. To keep your belongings safe, it's a good idea to pack a money belt or a secure travel wallet. During day trips and walks, a lightweight daypack or backpack comes in helpful for carrying your supplies.

Always remember to pack efficiently and lightly. Give yourself room in your suitcase for any trinkets or mementos you find along the trip. You'll be well-prepared to enjoy your trip journey in the Philippines if you adhere to these packing suggestions and take into account the necessities listed above. Happy travels!

PHILIPPINES TRAVEL GUIDE 2023

CHAPTER FOUR

Manila: The Capital

Exploring the City's Historic Sites

The energetic, culturally diverse, and historically significant capital of the Philippines is Manila. This busy metropolis offers a fascinating fusion of the old and the new. In this section, we'll take you on a tour of some of Manila's most important historical monuments so you can learn more about the city's interesting history.

The Walled City, Intramuros

The center of old Manila, Intramuros, is where we first stop. This walled city, which was constructed during the Spanish colonial era, transports you back in time with its cobblestone streets, well-preserved buildings, and enchanting Spanish-style architecture. Fort Santiago, a former fortification turned national shrine, is a good place to start your trip. Visit Casa Manila, a gorgeously restored colonial home that offers an insight into the lavish lifestyle of the Spanish aristocracy, then take a leisurely stroll along the city walls. Don't miss the UNESCO World Heritage-listed San Agustin Church, which is renowned for its elaborate Baroque architecture and beautiful interiors.

A Tribute to the National Hero: Rizal Park

Our next stop is Rizal Park, a vast green haven honoring Dr. Jose Rizal, the national hero of the Philippines. Investigate the park's vast grounds, which are decorated with statues, fountains, and well-kept gardens. Visit the Rizal Monument, an imposing sculpture made of bronze that serves as a representation of liberty and nationalism. The National Museum of Fine Arts and the National Museum of Anthropology are nearby institutions that house a variety of artistic and historical treasures.

The oldest Chinatown is in Binondo.

The oldest Chinatown in the world, Binondo, must be seen during every trip to Manila. Immerse yourself in its bustling streets, which are dotted with authentic Chinese eateries, stores, and temples. Explore Binondo's cuisine scene, which is renowned for its mouthwatering dim sum, noodles, and regional Chinese-Filipino dishes, to delight your taste buds. The renowned Binondo Church is a masterwork of architecture that combines Chinese and European influences.

Malacaang Palace: The Center of Authority

Visit Malacaang Palace to get an insight into the political past of the Philippines. Throughout the history of the country, several important events have taken place in this opulent presidential home. Even though there isn't much access for the public inside, you may still admire the building's stunning exterior and wander the grounds. Visit the Malacaang Museum, which features relics, mementos, and works of art that offer insights into the political climate of the nation.

Church in San Sebastian: A Steel Wonder

Explore the Quiapo neighborhood to see San Sebastian Church's distinctive charm. This Gothic Revival masterpiece stands out as the only all-steel church in Asia and is an exquisite example of the style. Enter and be amazed by the elaborate interiors and beautiful stained glass windows. You will undoubtedly be in awe of this extraordinary church's structural inventiveness and historical significance after visiting it.

Spend some time talking to locals, enjoying the flavors of Filipino food, and taking in the lively ambiance of the city as you tour these historic locations in Manila. These recognizable sites will provide you with a glimpse into the city's past and leave you with a great appreciation for its cultural fabric, whether you're a history enthusiast, an architecture lover, or simply interested in Manila's rich heritage.

Prior to your visit, don't forget to verify the most recent travel warnings and closing times for each location as times may change. Prepare to set out on an incredible adventure through Manila's historic monuments, where the old and the new mix peacefully to create a city that is genuinely alive with tales from the past.

Iconic Landmark & Attractions

Manila, a dynamic metropolis, offers a fascinating fusion of a long history, numerous cultural traditions, and contemporary advancements. This section will examine some of the recognizable landmarks and tourist hotspots that make Manila a must-visit location for tourists from all over the world.

Intramuros: Entering the Past

Intramuros, a historic walled city from the Spanish colonial era, serves as the starting point of our tour of Manila. Explore the historic fortifications, churches, and cobblestone streets to immerse yourself in a bygone age. Visit the historical site of Fort Santiago, where Dr. Jose Rizal, a national hero, was held before being put to death. Discover the fascinating tales that shaped the Philippines while letting yourself be swept up in the enchantment of this living museum.

A Tribute to the National Hero: Rizal Park

Rizal Park, a sizable urban oasis honoring Dr. Jose Rizal, is located close to Intramuros. This famous park offers a tranquil retreat from the bustle of the city. Enjoy a leisurely stroll through the lush vegetation, marvel at the elaborate gardens, and find statues and monuments honoring the nation's national hero. Rizal Park is a bustling hub for both locals and tourists since it serves as both a calm retreat and a location for cultural activities and meetings.

Dive into the Marine Wonders at Manila Ocean Park

Visit Manila Ocean Park, which is situated in Manila Bay, for an exciting underwater journey. Visitors of all ages can have a captivating experience at this top-notch aquatic theme park. Enjoy the breathtaking underwater tunnel while taking in the vibrant assortment of aquatic life swimming above you. Enjoy engaging displays, exciting performances, and even the chance to swim with whale sharks, which are gentle giants. Nature lovers and those looking for an amazing marine experience can not miss Manila Ocean Park.

Philippine National Museum: A Cultural Treasure Vault

Visit the National Museum of the Philippines to indulge in the rich cultural legacy of the country. This esteemed institution is home to a sizable collection of works of art, relics, and historical treasures. View the masterpieces created by renowned Filipino artists Juan Luna and Fernando Amorsolo at the National Art

Gallery. Learn about the various cultures that influenced the archipelago by exploring the archaeological and anthropological collections. The nation's aesthetic and historical heritage is exemplified through the National Museum.

Sunset over Manila Bay: A Magnificent Display

The breathtaking sunset in Manila Bay is a must-see on any trip to Manila. Go to the Baywalk area, locate a cozy position, and watch as the sun sets and the sky bursts into brilliant colors. The silhouettes of Manila's famous buildings, like the Manila Baywalk, the Cultural Center of the Philippines, and the Manila Yacht Club, add even more nostalgia to the sunset vista. Take pictures of this unforgettable moment to save your memories of the city.

Binondo: The Oldest Chinatown in the World

Explore Binondo's bustling streets to experience the energetic ambiance of the world's oldest Chinatown. Experience a culinary adventure as you try delicious dumplings and luscious roast ducks from real Chinese cuisine. Discover the quaint stores selling a variety of items, such as herbs, tea, and strange foods, that line the small lanes. Don't forget to check out the famous Binondo Church, which serves as a symbol of the Chinese and Filipino ancestry that still lives in this area.

The Philippines' vivacious capital, Manila, offers a mesmerizing fusion of natural beauty, history, and culture. Every famous site and attraction, from the guarded Intramuros walls to the romantic Manila Bay sunset, tells a tale that embodies the spirit of the country. Immerse yourself in Manila's charm and energy, and let its diverse array of experiences leave a lasting impression on your vacation memories.

Culinary Delights & Local Cuisine

Manila provides a delectable variety of gastronomic delights that will leave your taste buds hankering for more in addition to a vivid blend of history, culture, and modernity. Manila is a sanctuary for food lovers looking for a culinary journey, offering both local Filipino cuisine and delicacies from around the world. Let's explore the fascinating and varied world of Manila's regional cuisine.

An Aromatic Tapestry

The cuisine of Manila is a tapestry made of a diverse fusion of local flavors, Spanish influences, Chinese culinary customs, and contemporary fusion dishes. Filipino food is renowned for its strong flavors that frequently combine sweet, sour, and savory ingredients.

It's a delicious clash of flavors that honors the nation's varied past and history.

Specialty Dishes

You must try a few of Manila's iconic dishes when visiting the city's culinary scene. Adobo is a savory blend of meat (often pork or chicken) marinated in vinegar, soy sauce, garlic, and spices, then cooked to perfection. It is sometimes regarded as the national cuisine of the Philippines. Sinigang, a sour soup filled with tamarind, tomatoes, and different veggies, is another dish you should try. You may serve it with your choice of meat or seafood. Not to be forgotten is the legendary lechon, a whole roasted pig with crispy skin and tender meat that is frequently the focal point of festive gatherings.

Markets and Hawker Centers for Food

Visit Manila's hopping food markets and hawker centers to get a taste of the colorful local cuisine culture. Mercato Centrale in Bonifacio is one such well-liked location. Street food, cosmopolitan cuisine, and cutting-edge food concepts may all be found at Global City. It's the ideal place to enjoy a wide range of Filipino cuisine, from traditional favorites to contemporary takes, thanks to the fragrances, colors, and lively ambiance.

Chinatown: A Foodie Mecca

Binondo, or Chinatown in Manila, is a foodie's dream come true. A wide variety of Chinese and Filipino foods are served at the many Chinese restaurants and small cafes that dot this thriving neighborhood. Enjoy mouthwatering dim sum, delicious roasted duck, or scorching hot bowls of beef noodle soup. Try the hopia, a sweet pastry filled with mung beans or other delectable fillings, as well as the well-known fried siopao, a fluffy bun filled with savory pig filling.

Sweets from the Street

Manila's culinary environment cannot be fully appreciated without experiencing its thriving street food scene. Food stalls and sellers selling a variety of savory appetizers and sweet delights make the streets bustle. Try the popular balut, a fertilized duck embryo boiled and eaten as a snack, or the fish balls, skewered and deep-fried fish balls served with a variety of sauces. Enjoy a colorful dessert called halo-halo, which is made of crushed ice, sweetened fruits, jelly, beans, and leche flan and is served with a scoop of ice cream and evaporated milk on top.

Filipino cuisine now

Although Manila's cuisine places a specific emphasis on traditional foods, there is also a thriving modern food movement in the city. Filipino cuisine is being reimagined by creative chefs and eateries, who are merging it with modern methods and other inspirations.

At well-known eateries like Toyo Eatery, Gallery by Chele, or Hey Handsome, you may sample upgraded Filipino dishes with a contemporary touch.

Taking care of your sweet tooth

Filipinos unquestionably enjoy sweets, and Manila has a wide selection of delectable desserts to satiate your sweet craving. The sticky bliss of biko, a sweet rice cake cooked in coconut milk and brown sugar, or sink your teeth into a warm bibingka, a rice cake covered with butter and grated coconut. If you're in the mood for something cool and sour, try the calamansi tart, which is produced from the citrus fruit found in the area.

Don't pass up the chance to go on a culinary adventure as you see the colorful metropolis of Manila. The city's culinary culture will leave you with enduring memories and a renewed respect for the varied and delectable Filipino cuisine, from classic flavors to creative fusion concoctions. Take advantage of Manila's rich gastronomic offerings and indulge in the sensory feast.

Shopping & Entertainment Options

In this section, we'll look at the countless retail and leisure opportunities that make Manila a paradise for both natives and visitors. Manila offers something for everyone, from expansive malls to bustling marketplaces and from historical performances to cutting-edge attractions.

Shopping Paradise: With a vast variety of stores that can accommodate all preferences and price ranges, Manila is a shopaholic's paradise. Let's look at some of the most well-liked shopping areas in the city:

SM Mall of Asia: The SM Mall of Asia (MOA), one of the biggest malls in Asia, is a shopper's paradise. The MOA is home to hundreds of shops, from exclusive boutiques to low-cost fashion retailers. In addition to shopping, there are other entertainment alternatives available, such as an IMAX cinema, an ice skating rink, and a range of dining establishments.

Greenbelt Mall: Sophisticated shopping center with a mix of domestic and foreign brands, Greenbelt Mall is situated in Makati's affluent area. The mall has lush gardens and outdoor patios, and it is exquisitely designed. Modern home design shops, upscale clothing businesses, and fine eating establishments can all be found here.

For those looking for a more affordable shopping experience, Divisoria Market is the place to go. This crowded market, which is well-known for its low prices, is a veritable gold mine of inexpensive clothing, accessories, toys, and household goods. Explore the confusing streets filled with kiosks selling a range of things and be ready to bargain with vendors.

Extravagant Entertainment: Manila is also recognized for its thriving entertainment scene, where guests may immerse themselves in top-notch shows, exhilarating amusement parks, and cultural performances. Here are some of the city's top attractions for entertainment:

Philippine Cultural Center (CCP):

The CCP, the country's foremost performing arts facility, presents a wide variety of local and foreign talent. Visitors may get a taste of the diversity of Philippine culture through exciting performances, which range from ballet and classical music to theater and modern dance. To catch a program that appeals to you, check the schedule in advance.

Resorts World Manila: This entertainment complex, which is close to the airport, has a full range of activities. It has a casino, opulent hotels, upscale stores, and a variety of fine dining establishments. The Newport Performing Arts Theater also presents top-notch performances, such as Broadway musicals and concerts by international musicians.

The Enchanted Kingdom is the ideal vacation spot for both families and thrill-seekers. This amusement park, which is not far from Manila, features a variety of thrilling rides and other activities for visitors of all ages.

Visitors can have a fun-filled day full of adventure and heart-pounding roller coasters at these theme parks.

In terms of being a bustling city with a wide variety of shopping and leisure opportunities, Manila truly lives up to its name. This vibrant city has something for everyone, whether you're a fan of fashion, a lover of culture, or just looking for some excitement. Manila makes sure that guests have a wonderful trip loaded with shopping, entertainment, and unlimited fun, from posh malls to bustling markets and from top-notch shows to exhilarating amusement parks. So gather your shopping bags and get ready to embrace Manila's vibrant energy!

PHILIPPINES TRAVEL GUIDE 2023

CHAPTER FIVE

Island Hopping

Popular Island Destinations & Their Unique Features

With more than 7,000 islands, the Philippines is a tropical paradise that presents a wide range of chances for island-hopping enthusiasts. Each island has a unique charm, amazing natural features, and rich cultural history. In this section, we'll examine seven of the Philippines' most well-known islands and emphasize their distinctive qualities, which make them must-see locations for any traveler.

The Last Frontier: Palawan

Palawan, dubbed "The Last Frontier" of the Philippines, is a true treasure. It is the location of the alluring Bacuit Archipelago, which boasts limestone cliffs, azure waters, and undiscovered lagoons. In Palawan, El Nido and Coron are two well-liked starting sites for island hopping. You can explore the underwater wonderland of Coron's shipwrecks and brilliant coral reefs or go to El Nido's captivating Big and Small Lagoons.

A Tropical Playground: Boracay

For its breathtaking White Beach, which is regarded as one of the best beaches in the world, Boracay Island has attracted attention from all over the world. Beyond its fine sands and beautiful waters, Boracay provides a variety of water sports, including kiteboarding, parasailing, and snorkeling. Visit Puka Beach for a more relaxed experience, or travel to surrounding islands like Carabao Island for a more sedate shoreline.

Cebu: A Wonderland of Culture and Water

Cebu is a hub of activity and a starting point for trips to stunning island getaways. Start your island-hopping journey on Mactan Island, which is renowned for its top-notch diving locations. Seize the chance to swim among gentle giants in Oslob's whale shark viewing area. Visit the lovely Kawasan Falls in Badian or travel farther south to discover the charming Bantayan and Malapascua islands.

Siargao: The Home of Surfing

Siargao Island, known for its world-class waves and laid-back atmosphere, is a surfer's dream. The renowned surf spot Cloud 9, which is situated in General Luna, draws surfers from all around the world. But Siargao offers more than just surfing. When you go island hopping in Siargao, you'll visit surrounding islands like Guyam, Daku, and Naked Island where you can relax in the sun, swim in crystal-clear waters, and eat delicious seafood.

Bohol: The Playground of Nature

Bohol is a tropical paradise gifted with a variety of natural beauties and scenery. It's breathtaking to see the cone-shaped hills known as the Chocolate Hills. Visit a floating restaurant while on a river tour along the Loboc River and take in the gorgeous surroundings. Just off the coast of Bohol, Panglao Island is a well-liked diving and snorkeling location with thriving marine life and gorgeous coral reefs.

The Island Born of Fire is Camiguin.

Camiguin is a small island province known as the "Island Born of Fire," with a spectacular topography. Mount Hibok-Hibok, a volcano with exhilarating trekking chances, is located there. Natural attractions on the island include hot springs, waterfalls, and the alluring White Island, a spotless sandbar encircled by azure waters. Don't miss the opportunity to view the spectacular sunset from the remains of the former Guiob Church.

The Untouched Beauty of Batanes

The Batanes group of islands, which are situated in the far north of the Philippines, are a treasure waiting to be found. Its untamed scenery, sloping hills, and rocky coasts provide for a stunning scene. Visit the centuries-old stone homes on Sabtang Island, learn about Ivatan culture, and be amazed by the stunning views from the Basco Lighthouse.

These are just a few of the Philippines' numerous islands that you can visit. Each provides a distinctive experience and an opportunity to discover the natural splendor and lively culture of the nation. As you set out on your island-hopping vacation, keep in mind to preserve the environment, adopt sustainable habits, and respect native cultures. A true tropical paradise, the Philippines will capture your heart and leave you with priceless memories.

Beaches, Snorkeling, & Diving Spots

In the Philippines, island hopping is a thrilling experience that gives visitors a chance to see the nation's stunning beaches, abundant marine life, and fascinating undersea landscapes. The Philippines is a haven for beach lovers, snorkelers, and divers with over 7,000 islands dotting the archipelago. This section will reveal some of the best island-hopping locations that highlight the nation's natural beauties.

The Philippines' "Last Frontier," Palawan, is a must-visit location for island hopping. Start your tour in El Nido, where you'll find secluded beaches, pristine lagoons, and towering limestone cliffs. Visit well-known locations like Shimizu Island, Secret Lagoon, and the Big and Small Lagoons as you travel among the islands of the Bacuit Archipelago. For those who enjoy snorkeling and diving, Coron provides beautiful lakes, WWII shipwrecks, and vivid coral gardens.

Another treasure in the Philippines' island-hopping itinerary is Cebu. Start on Mactan Island, where you may go snorkeling next to vibrant coral reefs and see a variety of aquatic creatures. From there, travel to the nearby islands of Nalusuan and Pandanon, which are renowned for their immaculate shorelines and clear waters. Malapascua Island, a diving sanctuary well-known for the opportunity to swim with thresher sharks, is only a short boat ride away. Don't forget to take a refreshing bath in the thick jungle surroundings at the captivating Kawasan Falls in southern Cebu.

Bohol: Situated in the center of the Visayas area, Bohol provides a variety of cultural and natural beauties. Panglao Island, renowned for its white sand beaches and vivid coral reefs, is a great place to start your island-hopping experience. Discover Balicasag Island, a marine sanctuary ideal for snorkeling that is teaming with exotic fish and sea turtles. Don't pass up the opportunity to see the famous Chocolate Hills, a remarkable geological structure that will wow you.

Siargao: Siargao, known as the "Surfing Capital of the Philippines," is renowned worldwide for its top-notch waves. The island has picturesque islands and lovely lagoons but is most renowned for its surfing scene. Join an island-hopping tour and visit Guyam, Daku, and Naked Islands to take advantage of the gorgeous beaches, hammocks, and locally caught seafood. Visit the picturesque Sugba Lagoon, encircled by thick mangroves, where you may swim, kayak, and cliff jump for a memorable experience.

Camiguin: Camiguin, a little volcanic island in Mindanao's north, is a treasure just waiting to be discovered. As the "Island Born of Fire," it provides a distinctive island-hopping experience. Discover the mysterious Sunken Cemetery, a submerged cemetery that appeared as a result of a volcanic eruption. Visit Mantigue Island's marine sanctuary, where you may snorkel among colorful coral gardens and a variety of aquatic life. Take a leisurely plunge in the cold waters of Tuasan Falls, which are surrounded by lush vegetation, to cap off your island-hopping journey.

In the Philippines, island hopping is a unique experience that takes you to some of the most beautiful places on earth. Each island provides a distinctive combination of natural beauty and adventure, from the towering limestone cliffs of Palawan to the vivid coral reefs of Cebu and the surfing paradise of Siargao. The Philippines' island hopping experience will leave you in awe of its magnificent scenery and rich marine species, regardless of whether you enjoy the beach, snorkeling, or diving. So grab your snorkeling gear and pack your swimsuit to start an exciting tour across these tropical havens.

Island Hopping Itineraries & Activities

Island-hopping is a must-do activity for tourists since it gives you the chance to explore several islands, unwind on pristine beaches, and learn about the varied marine life that lives beneath the clear seas. We'll show you some of the most exciting island-hopping routes and activities in the Philippines in this section.

I. Palawan, The Philippines' Jewel

The region of Palawan, frequently referred to as the "Last Frontier" of the Philippines, is home to breathtaking limestone cliffs, azure lagoons, and alluring undiscovered beaches. You can go on a unique island-hopping experience here.

El Nio Touring the Islands:

The stunning karst formations of El Nido are a great place to start your tour. Take the well-known island-hopping cruise, which will take you to Miniloc Island's gorgeous lagoons, Entalula Island's remote beaches, and the mesmerizing Big and Small Lagoons. Visit Shimizu Island's vivid coral gardens while snorkeling, and don't miss the chance to visit Secret Beach, which is only accessible via a tiny gap in the limestone cliffs.

Coron Island Escapade: Travel to Coron to start an incredible island-hopping adventure. Dive into the hypnotic waters of Kayangan Lake, which are encircled by high cliffs and verdant trees. Learn about the fascinating Twin Lagoons, where two azure lagoons are connected by a tiny opening in a limestone wall. Snorkel among the colorful coral gardens of Siete Pecados Marine Park's Skeleton Wreck, a mysterious WWII Japanese shipwreck.

II. The Visayas: A Heavenly Region in the Center of the Philippines

The center Philippines' Visayas region is well known for its pure white-sand beaches, clean waterways, and abundant marine life. Two island-hopping trips you shouldn't skip are listed below:

Island of Bohol and Cebu-Hopping:

Before boarding a boat to the nearby Pescador Island, you can see the well-known Kawasan Falls in Cebu, where your experience can begin. Admire the vibrant marine life in the nearby coral reefs when you dive or snorkel alongside sea turtles. Travel to Bohol from Cebu and take a cruise along the Loboc River, which is bordered by lush tropical forests. Visit Balicasag Island for a chance to swim with dolphins and dive in the vivid coral gardens, and explore the stunning Chocolate Hills.

Embark on a voyage to the alluring island of Siquijor, renowned for its magical allure and unmatched natural beauty. Go to Salagdoong Beach and dive down the bluff into the clear waters there. Discover the enchanting Cambugahay Falls, where you can jump into natural pools while swinging from a rope. Don't pass up the chance to see local healers who have been using ancient mysticism for generations conduct traditional healing rites.

III. Siargao Island, a surfing haven.

Siargao Island is well known worldwide as a renowned surfing location, but there is much more to this island's beauty than just the surf. Here is a sample of the interesting island-hopping activities on the island:

Take a boat journey to the secluded Sugba Lagoon, which is bordered by luxuriant mangroves. Swim with stingless jellyfish and dive into the pristine waters. Paddleboard or kayak in the lagoon, and trek to the nearby panoramic lookout for breathtaking views of the neighboring islands.

National Park near Sohoton Cove:

Explore Sohoton Cove National Park's natural beauties. Navigate through tight passageways flanked by precipitous limestone cliffs that lead to hidden lagoons and caverns. During a nighttime swim, take in the special pleasure of swimming through the Enchanted Cave's dim corridors and observing the blue glow of the bioluminescent plankton.

In the Philippines, island hopping offers a variety of experiences to suit the preferences of every traveler. The Philippines has everything you might want, whether you're looking for the peace of secret beaches, the thrill of water sports, or the wonders of marine life. Each island offers a distinct opportunity for exploration and adventure because of its diverse archipelago. Set out on an island-hopping adventure and allow the Philippines' breathtaking natural beauty and welcoming culture to mesmerize you.

CHAPTER SIX

Adventure & Nature

Hiking & Trekking Trails

The Philippines is a haven for those who enjoy the outdoors. For those wanting a once-in-a-lifetime adventure, the nation offers a variety of hiking and trekking trails through its lush rainforests, majestic mountains, and magnificent scenery. Every type of hiker will find something to enjoy in the Philippines, from strenuous mountain summits to peaceful forest routes. In this section, we'll look at some of the most well-known hiking and trekking routes in the nation.

Mount Pulag in Luzon

The third-highest mountain in the Philippines is Mt. Pulag, which is situated in the country's north and has a height of 2,926 meters. Beginners will find the Ambangeg Trail, which leads to the peak, to be a reasonably simple hike. You will be rewarded with breathtaking views of the nearby Cordillera Mountains as you ascend through mossy forests and grasslands. Experienced hikers looking for a more difficult journey can take the Akiki Trail, which is renowned for its difficult terrain and steep ascents.

Luzon's Taal Volcano is a noteworthy trekking location. It is tucked away in the province of Batangas. This volcano is spectacular since it is located on an island within a lake. The journey begins with a boat ride across the lake, then a short ascent to the volcano's crater on foot. When you reach the summit, a bizarre scene with a lake in the middle of a little active volcano will be seen. For nature lovers, this hike is a must-try because of the amazing views.

Mindanao's Mount Apo:

The tallest peak in the Philippines, Mount Apo, rises to a height of 2,954 meters and is a well-known hiking destination. The Kapatagan Trail, which leads to its summit, provides a difficult but worthwhile journey. You'll come across a variety of flora and fauna as you move through deep forests and mossy slopes. Hikers are rewarded with stunning panoramas at the summit, including the captivating dawn over the clouds.

Romblon's Mount Guiting-Guiting:

Sibuyan Island's Mount Guiting-Guiting is an exhilarating excursion for seasoned and expert hikers. The trail to the summit is only accessible by people with mountaineering expertise due to its rugged peaks and challenging landscape. The hike is a true test of stamina and bravery because it involves scrambling, rock climbing, and rappelling. The peak, however, provides magnificent views of the neighboring islands and the great ocean, so the effort is worthwhile.

Mount Pinatubo, on the island of Luzon: Famous for its disastrous explosion in 1991, Mount Pinatubo is now a well-liked hiking location. The 4x4 journey across the lahar-covered terrain on the trail to the crater lake is followed by a hike through difficult terrain. A mesmerizing scene is created by the crater lake's strange blue waters and the surrounding high cliffs. The hike is manageable for novices or those looking for a less strenuous excursion.

Although not a conventional hiking track, the Batad Rice Terraces in the province of Ifugao offer a distinctive and beautiful trekking experience. The cascading scene created by these terraces in the slope is recognized as a UNESCO World Heritage Site. The trip gives you a look into the rich cultural history of the Ifugao people as it passes past gorgeous towns, verdant rice fields, and magnificent vistas.

The Philippines boasts a variety of hiking and trekking trails to satisfy your appetite for outdoor discovery, whether you're an expert hiker or a first-time traveler. Each trail has its own distinctive beauty and challenge, from the difficult summits of Mount Apo and Mount Guiting-Guiting to the unusual vistas of Taal Volcano and Batad Rice Terraces. Prepare for an exciting voyage across the beautiful natural beauties of the Philippines by lacing up your hiking boots, packing your backpack, and heading off.

Volcanos Exploration

The Philippines is a place of many natural beauties, but its beautiful volcanoes are among its most alluring attractions. Volcano exploration provides intrepid travelers with an exhilarating and distinctive experience because of the archipelago's more than 20 active volcanoes. This section will walk you through the exhilarating realm of volcano exploration in the Philippines, including hiking to crater lakes and viewing explosions from a safe distance.

A Volcanic Paradise: The Ring of Fire

The Pacific Ring of Fire, where the Philippines are located, is noted for its severe volcanic and seismic activity. The geography of the nation has been molded by this geological hotspot, which has produced a wide variety of volcanoes, both dormant and active. The Taal Volcano in Batangas, Mount Pinatubo in Zambales, and Mount Mayon in Albay are a few of the most well-known volcanic locations in the Philippines. Those who want adventure will find opportunities for exhilarating exploration among these spectacular peaks.

Volcano monitoring and safety precautions: safety first

Prioritizing safety is vital before starting any volcano exploration excursion. In the entire nation, volcanic activity is regularly monitored by the Philippine Institute of Volcanology and Seismology (PHIVOLCS), which also promptly provides advisories and warnings. Always keep up with the most recent developments and follow any guidelines or advice issued by the authorities. Additionally, it is a good idea to engage a local guide who is knowledgeable about the region and can guarantee your safety while on the walk.

Trekking Volcanic Trails for Majestic Ascents

The main method for discovering the Philippines' volcanoes is hiking. With various levels of difficulty and time, each volcano offers a distinctive trekking experience. For experienced hikers, Mount Mayon, famed for its flawless cone shape, is a difficult yet worthwhile ascent. The hike to Mount Pinatubo, on the other hand, is considerably simpler and offers breathtaking scenery, including a magnificent crater lake. Visitors can climb to the crater rim of Taal Volcano, which has a distinctive location on an island within a lake, and see the breathtaking sight of molten lava below.

Hidden Gems in Volcanic Calderas at Crater Lakes

In the Philippines, many volcanoes have captivating crater lakes tucked away inside their calderas. These alluring sources of water provide a tranquil haven and are frequently encircled by luxuriant flora. One such instance is Negros Occidental's Mount Kanlaon, which has a stunning crater lake called Lake Silay. Another place to visit is Mount Apo in Mindanao, which has the highest peak in the nation and a gorgeous crater lake called Lake Venado. A chance for rest and introspection amidst the natural beauty of the volcano is offered by these lakes.

Volcanic Hot Springs: A Way to Unwind in Nature

Natural hot springs are also created by volcanic action, offering a singular way to unwind. Indulging in the healing waters of these hot springs is the ideal way to relax after a strenuous climb or expedition. The Albay hamlet of Tiwi is well-known for its geothermal springs, where guests can relax in healing waters surrounded by luxuriant vegetation. Similar to this, the Mount Pinatubo region has a number of hot spring resorts where visitors may relax their aching muscles in warm, mineral-rich pools.

Experiences with Eruption: Observing Volcanic Activity

Witnessing volcanic activity is an unforgettable experience for the truly daring. However, safety should always come first, and it is important to abide by local authorities instructions. Volcanic eruptions are best observed from a safe distance, in one of the approved viewing places or observation decks that are available. Visitors are frequently drawn to Mount Mayon by its periodic eruptions because they want to see the blazing show from a safe distance.

Exploring volcanoes in the Philippines mixes nature, adventure, and the majestic forces of the planet. The nation's volcanic wonders offer a singular experience for adventure-seeking tourists, with thrilling volcano explosions, strenuous climbs, tranquil crater lakes, and more. However, always put safety first, heed local authorities advice, and keep in mind that volcanic activity is always changing. So prepare your trekking boots, camera, and sense of adventure for an incredible journey into the volcanic splendor of the Philippines.

Waterfalls & Natural Wonders

For those who enjoy nature and adventure, the Philippines is a paradise. This archipelago offers a variety of options to explore and immerse yourself in its pristine beauty, from gushing waterfalls to spectacular natural wonders. We will explore some of the most beautiful waterfalls and other natural wonders the Philippines has to offer in this section.

imposing waterfalls

The Philippines is endowed with a profusion of magnificent waterfalls that will make you marvel at the strength and beauty of nature. Pagsanjan Falls, which can be found in the province of Laguna, is one such waterfall. This three-tiered waterfall, which is reachable through an exhilarating boat journey up the Pagsanjan River, drops into an emerald pool that is surrounded by lush vegetation. As you take in this natural wonder's overwhelming power and magnificence, get ready to be showered in the mist.

Kawasan Falls, which is tucked away in Cebu's woods, is another must-see waterfall. Kawasan Falls, a multi-level cascade that offers a soothing getaway for travelers, is renowned for its turquoise blue waters. Try canyoneering, an adrenaline activity that involves jumping, sliding, and rappelling down the waterfalls, or take a dip in the cold waters and swim with colorful fish.

Underground Rivers and Caves: There are a number of amazing underground rivers and caves in the Philippines that provide a look into an ethereal underground realm. One of the longest navigable underground rivers in the world can be found in Palawan's Puerto Princesa Subterranean River National Park, a UNESCO World Heritage Site. Take a paddleboat into this mysterious underground world and explore the limestone formations and rare creatures that are there.

Sagada, which is in the Mountain Province, is well known for having complex cave networks. The "Big Cave," also known as Sumaguing Cave, is home to breathtaking stalactites and stalagmites, as well as underground lakes and waterfalls. When you crawl through tight spaces and into hidden chambers on a hard spelunking trip, it's an experience unlike any other for the brave.

The mysterious Banaue Rice Terraces, frequently referred to as the "Eighth Wonder of the World," are located in the Philippines. These terraces, which ancient indigenous civilizations carved into the Ifugao mountains, are a prime example of the Filipino people's brilliant technical prowess. Be in awe of the size and accuracy of these cascading fields, which not only create a stunning panorama but also demonstrate sustainable agricultural methods.

Exploring the volcanic beauties of the Philippines is a great adventure for anyone who enjoys the outdoors. Located in Central Luzon, Mount Pinatubo provides a strenuous yet rewarding walk that leads to the rim of its breathtaking crater lake. The trip begins with a 4x4 ride over tough terrain and continues with a stroll through ash-covered valleys, revealing the ruins of the volcano's devastating 1991 eruption.

The Taal Volcano, which is located in Batangas, is another must-see volcanic location. Taal Volcano, one of the smallest active volcanoes in the world, has a beautiful crater lake that is appropriately known as the "Lake within a Lake." Obtain a panoramic view of the crater and its surroundings by hiking up to the rim of the volcano island after taking a boat journey there.

Amazing Coral Reefs: The Philippines is home to a variety of marine life and a lively underwater wonderland. The Sulu Sea's Tubbataha Reefs Natural Park, a UNESCO World Heritage Site, is one of the most well-known diving locations. Dive into the park's beautiful coral gardens to explore them, meet majestic manta rays, and swim with schools of vibrant fish. Even the most experienced divers will be in awe at Tubbataha Reefs' astounding richness.

The Philippines is a veritable gold mine of adventure and natural beauty, with everything from famous rice terraces and underground rivers to cascading waterfalls. Let the Philippines fascinate you with its beautiful vistas and unrivaled biodiversity as you immerse yourself in the splendor of these lovely locations. Whether you seek heart-pounding thrills or serene nature experiences, the Philippines will leave a lasting impression on your soul and provide lifelong memories.

Wildlife & Marine Sanctuaries

In the country, adventurers and environment lovers will both discover a haven where they may explore marine reserves and wildlife sanctuaries that are alive with life. This section will take you on a tour of some of the Philippines' most amazing marine and wildlife reserves.

One of the most well-known marine sanctuaries in the world is Tubbataha Reefs Natural Park, which is situated in the Sulu Sea and is a UNESCO World Heritage Site. It supports a diverse range of marine life, including more than 600 fish species, 360 coral types, whales, dolphins, sharks, and turtles. You may see the brilliant hues and diverse fauna that coexist beneath the surface of the pristine waters here by snorkeling and scuba diving.

Rice terraces in Banaue: Not all types of fauna and natural treasures can be found in the ocean. The Banaue Rice Terraces, sometimes referred to as the "Eighth Wonder of the World," is evidence of the creativity and skill of the native Ifugao people. These historic terraces, which were more than 2,000 years old and carved into the slope, provide stunning views and a chance to fully experience Philippine culture. Hike through the towns and terraces, getting to know the residents and discovering their customary farming methods.

Toffee Hills:

The Chocolate Hills in Bohol, a true natural wonder, are made up of more than 1,200 precisely cone-shaped hills that become brown during the dry season and resemble enormous chocolate kisses. These geological features produce a fantastical and alluring landscape. Explore the Chocolate Hills Complex where you may take a trip down the Loboc River to take in its magnificence from a different angle or for an extensive view, climb one of the slopes to the top.

Explore the Puerto Princesa Subterranean River National Park, which is home to the renowned Palawan Underground River, and descend into the earth's interior. This river is navigable and flows through a breathtaking limestone cave with magnificent stalactites and stalagmites for about 8.2 kilometers. Keep a look out for diverse bat species, monkeys, and other unusual fauna that call this subterranean environment their home as you float along the river on a paddleboat trip.

Whale Shark Interaction in Donsol: The province of Sorsogon's Donsol is dubbed the "Whale Shark Capital of the World." These gentle giants travel to the area between the months of November and June, giving tourists a once-in-a-lifetime chance to swim and connect with these majestic creatures. Join a responsible whale shark encounter trip to experience this incredible animal's size and elegance while also supporting conservation efforts.

Off the coast of Negros Oriental sits Apo Island, a marine sanctuary renowned for its beautiful coral reefs and a wealth of marine life. Explore the clean seas around the island while snorkeling or scuba diving with sea turtles, colorful fish, and other marine life. The island's ecosystem has been greatly protected by the local population, making it a shining example of effective community-based conservation.

Mt. Apo: The highest peak in the Philippines, Mount Apo, offers thrill-seekers and nature lovers an amazing experience. This magnificent mountain in Mindanao offers a variety of trails for hikers of all experience levels. You will see a variety of plants and animals, including the well-known Nepenthes or pitcher plants, as you rise. You are rewarded for reaching the summit with a wonderful panoramic view of the surroundings.

The Philippines' wildlife and marine reserves offer a rare chance to experience the natural beauty of the region up close. These sanctuaries will leave you with a strong respect for the nation's biodiversity and a desire to preserve these priceless ecosystems for future generations to enjoy, whether you're exploring the various marine life, hiking through historic terraces, or encountering gorgeous wildlife.

CHAPTER SEVEN

Local Cuisine & Dining

Popular Filipino Dishes & Street Food

In addition to its breathtaking beaches and energetic culture, the Philippines is a culinary heaven. Filipino cuisine is a delightful blend of several influences, such as Spanish, Chinese, Malay, and American food, creating a distinctive and varied food scene. This section will take you on a delightful journey through some of the most well-known Filipino cuisine and street food that you must sample when visiting the Philippines, from savory and hearty meals to delectable street food.

Adobo: Let's begin with the Filipino cuisine staple, adobo. This well-known meal consists of braised meat (often chicken or pork) that has been marinated in vinegar, soy sauce, garlic, and spices. Adobo is a favorite among both locals and visitors due to the marriage of acidic spices and delicate meat.

The sour soup known as sinigang nicely encapsulates the Filipinos' enjoyment of strong, bright flavors. The most popular souring agent is tamarind, however, other options include guava, calamansi, and green mango. Pork, shrimp, or fish are frequently included in this hearty soup, along with a variety of other veggies, to provide a wonderful and wholesome meal.

Lechon: For meat enthusiasts, lechon is a must-try because it is the king of Filipino celebrations. It is a whole roasted pig that has been spiced with a variety of seasonings to produce a crispy exterior and luscious meat. A long-standing custom, roasting the pig results in a distinctive flavor profile and a celebratory ambiance.

Kare-Kare:

Oxtail, tripe, or beef are cooked in a thick, creamy stew called kare-kare that has a peanut-based sauce. Bagoong, a fermented shrimp paste, is frequently served alongside this dish to give it a salty, flavorful edge. Kare-Kare's distinctive flavor combination is certain to leave a lasting impression and is best served with a serving of steaming rice.

Halo-Halo is a beloved Filipino delicacy that is both energizing and vibrant. This sweet dish is made out of a mixture of shaved ice, evaporated milk, various fruits, sweet beans, jellies, and leche flan. It's a delicious fusion of flavors and textures that offers a welcome break from the tropical heat.

Filipino street cuisine is a gourmet excursion all on its own, teasing your taste senses with a wide variety of flavors and textures. Here are some well-known foods from the street that you shouldn't miss:

Balut: This distinctively Filipino street cuisine may test your sense of adventure. It is boiling, shell-on embryonic duck that is being consumed. Although the blend of tastes and textures can take some getting used to, it's a must-try for anyone looking for a true street food experience.

Isaw: Isaw is the name for perfectly skewered and cooked chicken or pork intestines that have been barbecued. Before grilling, it is frequently marinated in a delicious sauce, producing a savory and slightly chewy appetizer. Isaw is frequently eaten with vinegar or hot sauce dip.

Fish Balls: In the Philippines, fish balls are a common street dish. These skewered, deep-fried balls of minced fish are served with a sweet and sour sauce. They are affordable, widely accessible, and ideal for a fast snack when traveling.

Kwek-Kwek: Kwek-Kwek is a well-liked street meal made from deep-fried, crispy hard-boiled quail eggs covered in an orange batter. These bite-sized sweets come with a vinegar-based dip and are both tasty and aesthetically pleasing.

A crucial component of any trip to the Philippines is sampling local cuisine and street food. This chapter has exposed you to some of the most well-known Filipino cuisines, from the Adobo, the country's national dish, to the savory delights of street food. Don't pass up the chance to experience the unique flavors, colorful ingredients, and culinary customs that make Filipino cuisine so unique. Grab your appetite, then get ready to embark on a culinary journey that will leave you wanting more.

Regional Specialties & Flavors

The Philippines is a culinary haven, with a wide variety of tastes and dishes that showcase its rich cultural heritage and geographic diversity. The regional cuisine is a tapestry of colorful tastes and unusual pairings, ranging from substantial stews to fresh seafood specialties. This section focuses on the regional specialties and tastes that make dining in the Philippines a genuinely unique experience.

Region of Luzon: The northern island of Luzon is home to many regional delicacies. Visitors may enjoy traditional Filipino fare like adobo (marinated beef in soy sauce and vinegar) and sinigang (tangy tamarind soup) in the busy capital city of Manila. The Ilocos region is well-known for its pinakbet (a vegetable stew made with shrimp paste) and bagnet (crispy fried pig belly). Meanwhile, the traditional foods pinuneg (blood sausage) and pinikpikan (chicken soup) are well-liked in the Cordillera Mountains.

Region of the Visayas: Situated in the center of the Philippines, the Visayas region provides a delectable selection of culinary delights. Lechon, a whole roasted pig with crispy skin and tender meat, is famous in Cebu, the "Queen City of the South," where it is produced in large quantities. A popular cuisine in Bacolod, Negros Occidental, is chicken inasal, which is grilled chicken that has been marinated in a unique mixture of spices. The fresh scallops, crabs, and prawns that can be found along the coast will also delight seafood aficionados.

The southernmost part of the Philippines, Mindanao, offers a distinctive fusion of tastes influenced by Malay, Indonesian, and Muslim traditions. Curacha, a species of deep-sea crab prized for its sweet and juicy meat, is a local delicacy in Zamboanga City. In Zamboanga and other parts of Mindanao, satti, a fiery broth prepared with beef or chicken skewers, is a common street meal. Durian is a bitter fruit with a creamy texture that is a contentious but well-known delicacy in Davao City.

Region of Bicol:

The southeastern area of Luzon, known as Bicol, is famous for its spicy and savory food. The must-try meal

Bicol Express, a fiery pig stew made with coconut milk and jalapeño peppers, exemplifies the love of strong flavors in the area. Another dish that showcases Bicolano culinary traditions is laing, which is formed from taro leaves that have been boiled in coconut milk and spices. Don't forget to try their distinctive chili pepper-based delicacy, sili ice cream!

The islands of the Visayas and Palawan:

Fresh seafood and exotic cuisines abound on the unspoiled islands of Palawan and the Visayas. The tamilok, a delicacy created from woodworms gathered from mangrove trees, is the most well-known meal in Palawan. You may sample the renowned kinilaw in Bohol, a raw fish dish seasoned in vinegar and herbs. Mangoes from Guimaras Island are well known for being among the sweetest in the world, making them the ideal component for cool sweets.

Exotic and Native Cuisines:

The Philippines offers a vast variety of native and exotic delicacies for food adventurers. The odd meal known as "tupig," a sticky rice cake wrapped in banana leaves and grilled over hot stones, originates from the Cordilleran mountains. You may try "camaru," or fried bugs, which are pleasantly crispy and tasty, in Pampanga. A rare delicacy called balut, which is a developing duck embryo cooked and consumed in its shell, may pique the interest of adventurous diners.

The Philippines' rich gastronomic landscape is revealed by traveling through the country's regional cuisines and flavors. Each bite narrates a tale of cultural history and regional traditions, from the savory stews of Luzon to the fiery cuisines of Bicol and the unique foods from diverse locations. The local cuisine and dining experiences in the Philippines will forever change your culinary journey, whether you're a foodie or just a curious traveler.

Dining Etiquette & Food Markets

The local eating scene, dining etiquette advice, and lively food markets that highlight the nation's culinary treasures will all be covered in this section.

Dining Etiquette: Filipinos are renowned for their gracious hospitality, and dining with locals is a great way to experience their sincere friendliness and generosity. Observe the following dining etiquette guidelines:

Esteem for seniors Respect for elders is a cornerstone of Filipino culture. Wait for the older Filipinos to begin eating before starting your meal when dining with them.

Use Utensils: Filipinos often use a spoon and fork to consume their meals. The fork is used to press food onto the spoon while the spoon is scooped up with the right hand. Knives are rarely employed until absolutely essential.

Dining the kamayan method: The kamayan, or "eating with your hands," is a traditional technique to eat food in the Philippines. If you are invited to a Kamayan-style lunch, wash your hands thoroughly before you eat and do as your hosts direct.

Filipino dinners are frequently served family-style, with several dishes arranged in the middle of the table. To ensure that everyone has a chance to sample each dish, it is usual to share food and eat minimal servings.

The host or cook should be complimented on the quality of the food; this is considered courteous. In Filipino dining customs, thanking and appreciating the food is a fundamental component of the meal.

Food Markets: Visiting food markets is a great way to get a taste of authentic Filipino cooking. These bustling markets offer a wide variety of fresh goods and fruit, as well as a window into the way of life in the area. Here are several well-known food markets you ought to go to:

Mercato Centrale, Manila: Mercato Centrale is a well-known food market that serves a wide variety of street cuisine and regional specialties. It is situated in the busy city of Manila. This market is a sanctuary for foodies, offering everything from traditional delicacies like adobo and lechon to cutting-edge culinary inventions.

Salcedo Saturday Market in Makati City is a great place to visit if you're in the city on a Saturday morning. This market is popular among both locals and foreigners alike and is well-known for its organic produce, artisanal food goods, and delicious street cuisine.

In Cebu City, Carbon Public Market is one of the biggest and oldest markets, and it is a sensory joy. This market is a treasure trove for intrepid food fans, offering a variety of seafood, tropical fruits, and spices as well as aromatic herbs and regional munchies.

Davao City's D'Bone Collector Museum and Market: The D'Bone Collector Museum and Market in Davao City exhibit a wonderful collection of animal bones and fossils while fusing education and food. You may sample regional cuisine and tropical fruits from the market kiosks while perusing the displays.

Negros Weekend Market, Bacolod City: Be sure to stop by the Negros Weekend Market if you're in Bacolod City over the weekend. This market, which is well-known for its delicious grilled specialties, sugarcane juice, and freshly baked pastries, is a sanctuary for gourmands looking for genuine Negrense delights.

The Philippines offers a culinary trip unlike any other, with everything from proper table manners to bustling food markets. Discover the vast range of ingredients in the regional food markets, appreciate the rich tapestry of flavors, and bask in the warmth of Filipino hospitality. The native cuisine will definitely leave you wanting more, whether you're savoring a traditional Kamayan feast or savoring street culinary treats.

CHAPTER EIGHT

Historical & Heritage Sites

UNESCO World Heritage Sites

Several of the Philippines' UNESCO World Heritage Sites offer a window into the country's past and highlight its distinctive traditions. In this section, we'll look at some of the most important historical and heritage locations that UNESCO has acknowledged for their exceptional universal importance.

Vigan's Historic City (1999):

The Historic City of Vigan, a well-preserved Spanish colonial town from the 16th century, is situated in the province of Ilocos Sur. Its historic homes, ancestral mansions, and cobblestone streets showcase a combination of Spanish, Chinese, and Filipino architectural traditions. For history fans and cultural lovers, the city's distinctive personality and historical significance make it a must-visit location.

Four churches from the Spanish era are included in the Baroque Churches of the Philippines (1993) UNESCO World Heritage Site, which may be found at Manila, Paoay, Miag-ao, and Santa Maria. These churches, which were constructed in the Spanish colonial era, exhibit a distinctive blend of European and Filipino architectural forms known as "Earthquake Baroque." The intricate designs, substantial buttresses, and elaborate façade of each church are evidence of the nation's strong Catholic tradition.

Rice Terraces of the Philippine Cordilleras (1995): The Rice Terraces of Banaue, Batad, Bangaan, Mayoyao, and Nagacadan are a wonder of ancient engineering and agricultural traditions, nestled in the hilly region of the Cordillera. These terraces, which the indigenous Ifugao people cut into the mountainside over 2,000 years ago, are still being used for farming today. This location is a fascinating monument to the nation's cultural legacy because of the harmonious coexistence of nature and human innovation.

Natural Park at the Tubbataha Reefs (1993):

The Tubbataha Reefs Natural Park, a protected marine ecosystem in the Sulu Sea, is renowned for its outstanding biodiversity and ecological importance. A remarkable variety of coral reefs threatened marine animals, and bright underwater vistas may be found at this UNESCO World Heritage Site. Divers from all over the world visit this protected region to discover the beauties of the undersea world and dive into its pristine waters.

National Park of the Subterranean River in Puerto Princesa (1999):

One of the most extraordinary natural wonders in the world is the Puerto Princesa Subterranean River National Park, which is located on the Philippine island of Palawan. The underground river that flows through limestone caverns and creates a surreal underground environment is its most notable feature. The spectacular stalactite and stalagmite formations can be seen while taking a boat excursion along the river, where visitors may also see several species of bats and other wildlife.

These UNESCO World Heritage Sites are important for the Philippines' tourism sector in addition to having historical and cultural significance. They give tourists the chance to learn about the nation's history, take part in its many different cultures, and behold its breathtaking natural beauty. Each location adds to the rich tapestry of Philippine heritage, whether you're wandering the centuries-old alleyways of Vigan, admiring the delicate baroque architecture of the cathedrals, or taking in the breathtaking scenery of the rice terraces and marine parks.

Remember to treat these places with care and abide by any guidelines established to guarantee their preservation. It will help you better understand and appreciate the value of these UNESCO World Heritage Sites if you take the time to read about the regional cultures and traditions connected to them.

Museums & Historical Landmarks

The Philippines is a nation with a remarkable fusion of indigenous, Spanish, and American influences, making it rich in history and culture. Any visitor to this archipelago must include visiting the historical and heritage sites in their itinerary. In this section, we'll examine the wide range of historical sites and museums that provide a window into the Philippines' past and rich cultural legacy.

The Walled City, Intramuros

Without visiting Manila's ancient walled city of Intramuros, no trip to the Philippines would be complete. This well-preserved stronghold, built during the Spanish colonial period, takes visitors to the time of Spanish rule. Visit famous locations including Fort Santiago, Casa Manila, and San Agustin Church, a UNESCO World Heritage Site, while taking a leisurely stroll along the cobblestone streets. Experience the splendor of the past up close and admire the stunning architecture that makes Intramuros unique.

Philippine National Museum

The National Museum of the Philippines, which is situated in Manila, is a trove of information on the history, art, and culture of the country. The museum has an amazing collection of items, which includes historical artwork, ethnographic objects, and archaeological discoveries. Admire Juan Luna's masterwork "Spoliarium," which depicts the Roman gladiatorial arena. The National Museum provides a thorough tour of the nation's cultural legacy, from pre-colonial gold to modern art.

Museum at Ayala

The Ayala Museum, which is located in Makati City, features Philippine art, history, and culture. Its collection highlights pivotal episodes in Philippine history and ranges from pre-colonial times to the present. Investigate the dioramas that represent important occasions, such as the People Power Revolution and the Battle of Mactan. The museum also holds transient exhibitions and cultural activities, giving visitors a dynamic experience.

Museum in Banaue

The Banaue Museum, located in the stunning Cordillera Mountains, is devoted to preserving the Ifugao culture and the well-known Banaue Rice Terraces. Discover the complex farming methods used for years to produce these magnificent terraces, a UNESCO World Heritage Site. Visitors can see interactive exhibits, photographs, and traditional items on display at the museum, which highlights the close bond between the Ifugao people and their environment.

The Living Heritage of Vigan

Visit the city of Vigan in the Ilocos Sur province to be taken back in time. A UNESCO World Heritage Site, this well-preserved Spanish colonial town provides a window into the Hispanic history of the Philippines. Walk down Calle Crisologo, a street dotted with historic homes built in the 18th century. Visit the Syquia Mansion, which serves as a museum displaying the way of life of the aristocracy during the Spanish colonial era. It was once the ancestral home of former Philippine President Elpidio Quirino.

Sugbo Museum

Museo Sugbo, a former provincial jail turned museum, is located in Cebu City. This vast complex is home to a varied collection that details the history of Cebu and the nearby islands. Explore the galleries to see the displays on colonial history, anthropology, and archaeology. Insights into Cebu's past as a commerce center and its prominence during the Spanish colonial era are provided by Museo Sugbo, which provides an entertaining and educational tour through Cebu's past.

Remember to respect these locations as they serve as live reminders of the Philippines' rich history and cultural identity when you set out on your historical and heritage tour of the country. Spend some time talking to local curators and tour guides who are enthusiastic about imparting their knowledge. You will develop a deeper understanding of the vibrant past and enduring influence of the Philippines by immersing yourself in these museums and historical sites.

Spanish Colonial Architecture

The history of the Philippines is extensive and inextricably tied to its time as a Spanish colony. The archipelago was ruled by Spain for more than three centuries, which had a long-lasting effect on its customs, architecture, and culture. The Spanish colonial architecture found in the Philippines is evidence of this important historical era. This section will look into the historical and heritage locations that are spread around the nation and highlight the magnificent Spanish colonial architecture.

Various influences and traits

In the Philippines, Spanish colonial architecture is distinguished by a blending of native Filipino, Chinese, and European elements. The Spanish conquistadors imported architectural styles from their native country and modified them to fit the local environment and resources. Coral stones, adobe, and bricks were frequently used in this building style, along with elaborate carvings and sophisticated ironwork.

Intramuros, Manila: A trip to Intramuros, Manila's walled city, is a must for anybody studying Spanish colonial architecture in the Philippines. The capital of the Spanish colony during the late 16th century, Intramuros is home to some of the best-preserved examples of this architectural type. The San Agustin Church is a magnificent example of Baroque design and is a UNESCO World Heritage Site. Visitors are transported back in time by its ornately carved wooden doors, massive altar, and brilliant ceiling murals.

The city of Vigan, Ilocos Sur, is a live example of Spanish colonial architecture and is situated in the northern section of the island of Luzon. The city's remarkably well-preserved Spanish colonial buildings led to its designation as a UNESCO World Heritage Site. The main thoroughfare in Vigan, Calle Crisologo, is lined with ancestral homes that feature the well-known "bahay na bato" style of architecture. These homes have a wood upper story, capiz shell windows, and terracotta roof tiles, with a stone or brick bottom floor.

Church in Paoay, Ilocos Norte:

The Paoay Church, also known as the Saint Augustine Church, in Paoay, Ilocos Norte, is a classic example of

Spanish colonial architecture infused with Filipino and Chinese elements. In order to endure the frequent earthquakes in the area, this UNESCO World Heritage Site has immense buttresses supporting its thick coral stone walls. Its distinctive "earthquake baroque" design highlights the seamless fusion of indigenous and European architectural styles.

Bohol has a number of Spanish colonial churches that have withstood the test of time. The Central Visayas region's province of Bohol is an island. Examples are the Church of Our Lady of the Immaculate Conception in Baclayon and the Church of San Pedro Apostol in Loboc. Architecturally, these churches display a fusion of Baroque, Rococo, and Neoclassical styles. The churches are noteworthy heritage sites because of their interior religious objects, finely carved facades, and usage of coral stones.

Santa Ana Church in Pampanga is a prime example of a Spanish colonial church that has maintained its structural integrity over time. It is situated in the province of Pampanga. It was constructed in the late 18th century and has a magnificent exterior with exquisite reliefs and artistic elements. Beautiful religious artifacts and vintage wooden furniture may be found inside the church, offering a window into the past.

A fascinating fusion of native, Chinese, and European influences may be seen in the Spanish colonial architecture found in the Philippines. These historical treasures, which include the walled city of Intramuros in Manila and the well-preserved heritage sites of Vigan, Bohol, Ilocos, and Pampanga, provide a window into the nation's colonial history. Travelers can gain an appreciation for the architectural splendor, workmanship, and cultural relevance of the Spanish colonial era in the Philippines by exploring these locations.

CHAPTER NINE

Cultural Immersion

Indigenous Tribes & Cultural Experiences

Engaging with its native tribes is one of the best ways to fully experience its diverse past. Exploring these communities offers a rare chance to see a living link to the nation's historical past because there are over 100 recognized indigenous groups, each with its own unique customs, traditions, and languages. We shall examine the indigenous tribes of the Philippines in this section, highlighting certain cultural encounters that will enhance your travels.

Meeting the Igorots in the Cordillera Region: The Igorots are the most well-known of the indigenous tribes that call the Cordillera Region, which lies in the northern section of Luzon, home. The Igorots, who are well-known for their sophisticated agricultural methods, handwoven fabrics, and historic burial customs, can be encountered on a visit to the area. Participate in a traditional "caao" feast where you may sample delicious Igorot food and take in the ancient rituals performed to mark significant anniversaries and harvests.

Discovering the Ifugao Rice Terraces' Traditional Ways: The Ifugao Rice Terraces, a UNESCO World Heritage Site, is a remarkable example of the Ifugao people's technical prowess. Explore the remarkable irrigation systems that have supported their crops for more than 2,000 years as you stroll across the terraces. Interact with the villagers to learn about their terracing practices, native agricultural skills, and rice-growing traditions. Gain insight into the Ifugao way of life by taking part in a hands-on rice planting or harvesting activity.

Finding the Answers to the Mysteries of the Mangyan People

Visit the Mangyan people, an indigenous people with a profound connection to nature and ancestral spirits, on the island of Mindoro. Interact culturally with the Mangyan people, who are renowned for their fine handwoven fabrics, age-old music, and esoteric beliefs. Visit their communities, see their artistry, and participate in workshops where you may learn traditional weaving methods or watch native musical instruments being played live.

In Lake Sebu, the T'boli Culture is being uncovered:

The T'boli people's cultural center is Lake Sebu, which is situated in the province of South Cotabato. Immerse yourself in the vibrant T'boli customs, which feature distinctive beadwork, ornate brass ornaments, and T'nalak cloth that is influenced by dreams. Attend cultural events to see their distinctive dances and music, such as the captivating "T'boli S'lung" and "Hegalong" ensembles. A deeper understanding of the T'boli people's ties to nature and sense of self will emerge via interaction with them.

Going beyond the traditional tourist experience, exploring the indigenous tribes of the Philippines offers an enriching cultural immersion. Interacting with these groups offers a view into the diverse tapestry of customs, beliefs, and practices that make up the nation. Each encounter will leave you with a profound respect for the tenacity and distinctiveness of the indigenous tribes of the Philippines, whether it be taking part in an Igorot caao feast, exploring the Ifugao rice terraces, learning about the Mangyan people, or getting to know the vibrant T'boli culture. As you set out on a voyage of comprehension and connection with the heart and soul of the Philippines, embrace these cultural encounters, observe regional customs, and treasure the memories.

Festivals & Celebrations

Immersing yourself in the culture by taking part in the numerous festivals and celebrations that are held all around the archipelago is another way to make the most of your stay. These celebrations highlight the Filipinos' passion for cuisine, music, dance, and their ingrained religiosity. As you set off on a cultural tour unlike any other, join in the fun, take in the joyful festivities, and watch the vibrant parades.

Festival of Sinulog in Cebu City:

One of the most prestigious and lavish events in the Philippines is the Sinulog Festival, which takes place every January in Cebu City. It honors the Santo Nio (Child Jesus) and remembers the nation's conversion to Christianity. The celebration culminates in a mesmerizing street parade when participants parade and play drums to the music while dancing in exquisite attire. "Pit Seor!" is shouted down the street as people dance in stunning clothing and play drums to the music. The atmosphere is electrifying as residents and tourists assemble to watch this amazing performance.

Ati-Atihan Festival (Kalibo, Aklan): The Ati-Atihan Festival is a vibrant and joyous celebration that honors the native Ati people. It is held in January in Kalibo, Aklan. In an effort to emulate Ati's lifestyle, festival attendees cover their faces in black soot and dress in traditional tribal garb. As partygoers yell "Hala Bira!" and participate in street gatherings, the streets come alive with live music and dance. Don't pass up the opportunity to participate in the "Sadsad," a street dance.

The Pahiyas Festival, which takes place in May in Lucban, Quezon, is a stunning exhibition of creativity and appreciation for a plentiful harvest. The inhabitants utilize a variety of colorful rice cakes, fruits, vegetables, and handicrafts fashioned from coconut leaves and rice stalks to adorn their homes. The magnificent procession in which locals display their artistically decorated homes is a major attraction. Enjoy native treats like "Kiping," rice wafers molded into vibrant leaves and afterward baked into chips, as you take in this visual feast.

The Kadayawan Festival is a week-long Thanksgiving event held each August in Davao City that highlights the diverse cultural traditions of the local indigenous tribes. Enjoy the colorful parades, cultural performances, and food festivals. Don't pass up the opportunity to sample the exotic fruits, which are plentiful at this season, and include durian and pomelo. Witness the "Indak-Indak sa Kadalanan," a street dance competition where competitors fascinate the audience with their elegant dances while wearing traditional costumes.

The Panagbenga Festival, often known as the "Flower Festival," takes place in February in Baguio City, the Philippines' summer capital. Beautiful floats decorated with vibrant flowers parade through the streets during this month-long festival. As local and international competitors battle for the greatest float design, be amazed by the inventiveness and artistry on exhibit.

Street dancing, band concerts, and a spectacular fireworks show are all part of the celebrations.

These are but a few of the numerous festivals and events you can take part in in the Philippines. Every region has its own distinctive festivals that are based on the customs and cultures there. There is always a celebration to be found, whether it's the thrilling MassKara Festival in Bacolod, the jovial Pintados-Kasadyaan Festival in Tacloban, or the captivating Parada ng Lechon in Balayan.

Witnessing the heart and soul of the Filipino people while participating in these festivities and celebrations is possible. It's a chance to interact with locals, discover their traditions, and create priceless memories. Don't pass up this opportunity to soak up the festive splendor of the Philippines and the warmth and hospitality of its people.

Homestays & Community Based-Tourism

Immersion in the local culture and developing a deeper understanding of the people and their way of life are two of the most fulfilling travel experiences. In the Philippines, homestays and community-based tourism offer a singular chance for visitors to interact with local communities, discover their traditions, customs, and daily routines, and develop deep connections. The idea of cultural immersion through homestays and community-based tourism is explored in this section, which will also provide advice on how to get a genuine taste of Filipino culture.

A Gateway to Local Hospitality: Homestays

The best way to truly immerse yourself in a culture is to stay in a local's home. In the Philippines, homestays give visitors the opportunity to live with a host family and participate in their daily activities, meals, and stories. You can choose a setting that suits your interests because these accommodations can be located in rural villages, coastal towns, and even urban districts.

The advantages of homestays

Both the traveler and the host family profit greatly from homestays. It provides guests with an immersive experience that allows them to witness and take part in regional cultures and traditions first-hand. Authentic home-cooked meals can be sampled, local crafts and skills can be learned, and cultural events like traditional music or dance can be enjoyed. You may directly support the local economy and uplift the host community by staying in a house.

Selecting the Best Homestay:

Selecting the ideal homestay is crucial for a satisfying visit. Examine several options and read evaluations left by prior visitors. Take into account the surroundings, the available activities, and how well they align with your interests. You can learn more about a particular facet of the local culture by participating in homestays that specialize in particular pursuits like farming, fishing, or handicrafts.

Taking Part in Community-Based Tourism: Community-based tourism initiatives cover a larger spectrum of local community-involved activities than only homestays. These programs are frequently run by community cooperatives or non-governmental organizations (NGOs) in an effort to encourage sustainable travel and give locals job opportunities.

Investigating Activities for Community-Based Tourism:

Depending on the location, community-based tourism activities can vary substantially. You might get the chance to take part in community-led tours, go to nearby markets or schools, see customary rituals, or get involved in environmental conservation initiatives. These interactions create respect for the community's way of life and enhance intercultural communication.

It's important to practice responsible tourism when participating in homestays and community-based travel. Be cognizant of cultural sensitivity, respect the traditions and customs of the host community, and adhere to any instructions or rules given to you by your hosts. By reducing waste, saving resources, and promoting regional companies and craftspeople, adopt a sustainable mindset.

Cultural immersion has a favorable effect on the host communities in addition to enhancing traveler experiences through homestays and community-based tourism. You may directly support neighborhood families and initiatives, which will help their economy grow and maintain their cultural legacy. Better awareness of diversity can be fostered by the relationships you make and the knowledge you acquire while you are there.

Homestays and community-based tourism are transformative methods of experiencing the Philippines' culture. You go on a journey of discovery, forging relationships with the people, customs, and way of life of the host community, by choosing to stay with local families and taking part in activities that are organized by the community. Remember that the only way you can properly understand the Philippines' vast cultural diversity is through these genuine experiences.

CHAPTER TEN

Practical Travel Tips

Local Transportation Tips

Traveling throughout the Philippines' stunning archipelago is an essential part of the trip, which is in and of itself an adventure. The Philippines offers a wide variety of transportation alternatives to meet the demands of any traveler, from crowded cities to far-flung islands. Here are some crucial local transportation pointers to bear in mind to ensure a smooth and comfortable journey.

Jeepneys:

The jeepney is one of the most recognizable forms of transportation in the Philippines. These brightly colored, distinctively constructed cars represent the nation's culture. Jeepneys are a cheap and practical way to go about cities and towns. They function as shared taxis on predetermined routes. Be aware that jeepneys can become crowded, particularly during peak hours, so plan on a comfortable journey.

Tricycles: The tricycle is another well-liked mode of local transportation. Both urban and rural settings can be found using these three-wheeled vehicles. Tricycles act as short-distance taxis, transporting patrons between nearby locations or across small distances. Before beginning the trip, haggle over the cost with the driver because tricycles sometimes lack meters.

Buses are a safe and pleasant choice for lengthier trips between cities and provinces. Buses come in a variety of styles, from basic to luxurious or air-conditioned coaches. It's a good idea to purchase your ticket in advance, especially during periods of high travel demand, as bus terminals are typically found close to city centers.

Since the Philippines is home to thousands of islands, ferry and boat services are essential for inter-island transport. While smaller boats and outrigger canoes are available for shorter voyages and island-hopping excursions, ferries are frequently employed to connect major islands. Check the schedules in advance because they may change based on the time of year and the weather.

Trains: Although the Philippines' train network is not as vast as some other nations, it is nevertheless important to take into account particular routes. Trains run by the Philippine National Railways (PNR) connect Metro Manila with neighboring provinces. Additionally, there are scenic train trips available, such as the Bicol Express, which travels through beautiful scenery.

Ride-Hailing Apps like Grab:

Ride-hailing applications like Grab are popular and offer a practical means of transportation in significant cities like Manila, Cebu, and Davao. You only need to download the app, schedule a ride, and a driver will pick you up. These apps provide transparent fare estimation, and you may select from a variety of vehicles, such as cars and motorcycles.

Renting a Car, Motorcycle, or Bike: If you want more freedom and flexibility, renting a car, motorcycle, or bicycle can be a fantastic choice. Major cities and popular tourist locations provide car rental services. However, keep in mind that urban traffic might be crowded and that road signage in rural regions may not always be obvious.

Prudence and safety:

It's critical to put your safety first when utilizing local transportation in the Philippines. Be aware of your surroundings, avoid flashing expensive or huge quantities of cash, and avoid showing these things. Utilizing dependable, licensed transportation services is advised. It is preferable to get advice from a hotel or a reliable local if you are unsure about a vehicle or driver.

Time and Flexibility: Make sure to budget extra time for using local transportation when organizing your trip. It is possible for schedules to vary or be delayed, especially when the weather is bad. Accept "Filipino time" as a cultural norm and be ready to be adaptable with your ideas.

Knowing these local transportation hints will give you the assurance you need to move about the Philippines with efficiency and fully experience its rich culture. Never forget to enjoy the voyage and all that the Philippines has to offer, including its diverse scenery and friendly people.

Health & Safety Precautions

Prioritizing your health and safety is crucial when visiting the Philippines. Despite the country's stunning natural beauty and diverse culture, a smooth and enjoyable vacation can be achieved by being well-informed and prepared. This section offers a summary of significant health and safety concerns to take into account while you are there.

Water and Food Safety: It is advised to only drink bottled or filtered water to prevent gastrointestinal disorders. Avoid drinking beverages with unidentified water sources, ice cubes, and tap water. When eating out, pick establishments with reputable sanitary standards. To reduce the risk of foodborne infections, choose freshly prepared hot meals and peel fruits yourself.

Malaria and dengue fever are two mosquito-borne illnesses that can be found in the Philippines. Apply mosquito repellent with DEET or other appropriate components to protect yourself. When mosquitoes are most active, which is between dawn and night, wear light, long-sleeved clothing, and pants. Think about booking rooms with screens on the windows and doors or use insecticide-treated sleeping nets.

Sun protection: The Philippines' tropical climate means that there is a lot of sunshine, therefore it's important to shield oneself from dangerous UV rays. Wear a hat, use sunglasses, and apply sunscreen with a high SPF to protect your eyes. During the warmest parts of the day, seek cover and drink lots of water to stay hydrated.

Transportation and Traffic Safety:

Use caution when renting a car or taking the Philippines' public transportation system. Observe the traffic laws that apply in your area. If you intend to drive, make sure your international driver's license is current and educate yourself on the local driving customs. Traffic, especially in urban areas, can be unexpected, therefore use caution when crossing roadways.

Typhoons, earthquakes, and volcanic eruptions are among the natural disasters that the Philippines is prone to. Keep an eye on weather reports and pay attention to any cautions or warnings issued by local authorities. Learn how to evacuate in case of an emergency, and note down safe places to go. Keep vital papers and emergency contact information in a safe location.

Petty Crime and Personal Safety: Although most Filipinos are hospitable and kind, it is advisable to take security measures against petty crime. Keep an eye on your possessions, particularly when using public transportation or in crowded settings. Keep expensive objects hidden and use discretion when handling cash. Use ATMs that are well-lit and secure, particularly inside banks or retail establishments.

Travel insurance: It is highly advised that you buy comprehensive travel insurance for your trip to the Philippines. It ought to include personal liability, lost or stolen property, missed or interrupted travel, and medical crises. Examine the contract carefully to make sure it covers your unique needs, and think about buying insurance that offers medical evacuation protection.

Local Laws and Customs: To prevent inadvertent violations, familiarize oneself with local laws and customs. When visiting holy sites, dress modestly and keep in mind the cultural customs and sensitivities of the area. Keep a copy of your passport and other pertinent travel documents in your possession and store the originals somewhere safe.

You can more fully enjoy your trips in the Philippines if you are knowledgeable about health and safety concerns. To guarantee a memorable and safe journey, keep in mind to plan ahead, take the required precautions, and stay situationally aware.

Sustainable Travel Practices

The Philippines is a country blessed with incredible natural beauty, a wide range of ecosystems, and a deep cultural history. It is our duty as travelers to make sure that our travels have a positive effect on the environment, nearby communities, and the preservation of cultural traditions. We can help to ensure the long-term preservation of this stunning archipelago and the livelihoods of those who call it home by adopting sustainable travel habits. Here are some essential guidelines and pointers for pursuing environmentally friendly tourism in the Philippines.

The Philippines is home to a diverse range of plants and animals, including critically endangered species like the Philippine eagle and sea turtles. Follow appropriate animal-watching standards, such as keeping a safe distance and not harming their habitats, to preserve these natural gems. Instead of indulging in hobbies that exploit or damage animals, choose environmentally friendly ones like birdwatching, snorkeling, and hiking.

Reduce Plastic Waste: In the Philippines, plastic pollution is a serious environmental problem that notably affects the coastline and marine life. To reduce your plastic footprint, travel sustainably by packing a reusable water bottle, cloth shopping bags, and reusable silverware. Instead of purchasing bottled water, fill your water bottle at filtered water stations or purify your water with water purification tablets. Use the specified recycling bins or carry your trash with you until you find a suitable disposal facility to dispose of it responsibly.

Select judicious accommodations:

Support lodgings that place a high priority on sustainability and environmental friendliness. Look for hotels and resorts that use waste management programs, conservation techniques for water and energy, and renewable energy sources. Think about booking a stay at an eco-lodge, a homestay, or a community-based tourism project that directly benefits the neighborhood and helps to energize its local economy.

Accept the Community and Local Culture:

Participate in and show respect for the local communities traditions, customs, and way of life. Look for chances to meet locals through homestays, cultural excursions, or volunteer endeavors that advance local development. By supporting regional makers and aiding in the preservation of traditional crafts, buy locally created goods.

Select eco-friendly transportation:

Pick environmentally sustainable modes of transportation whenever possible. Use public transportation options like buses, jeepneys, and tricycles to help the neighborhood economy and minimize carbon emissions. Choose fuel-efficient or electric cars if you need to rent a vehicle. When traveling small distances, think about taking the pedestrian or bicycle route to reduce your carbon impact and to better get acquainted with the area.

Energy and resource conservation

While visiting the Philippines, make sure to use resources and energy responsibly. When not in use, turn off the lights, the air conditioner, and other electronics. Use reusable towels and take shorter showers to save water. Pick tour companies and locations that put an emphasis on sustainable methods, such as reducing their influence on the environment and assisting regional conservation initiatives.

Follow the "Leave No Trace" guidelines if you are exploring beautiful landscapes or pristine beaches. Take care to pack out all of your rubbish, show respect for plants and animals, and spare the delicate ecosystems. To help conserve these locations for future generations, leave major tourist destinations in the same condition that you found them, or even better, take part in coordinated cleanup efforts.

You can help the Philippines while enjoying the natural beauty and lively culture of the nation by implementing these sustainable travel habits. Let your journey be one that promotes environmental care, strengthens local communities, and aids in the preservation of this incredible place for future generations.

CONCLUSION

As we conclude our tour of the Philippines, we have a deep appreciation for the charm, variety, and friendliness of this alluring archipelago. For visitors looking for adventure, leisure, and cultural immersion, the Philippines provides a variety of amazing experiences, from beautiful beaches and crystal-clear oceans to verdant mountains and dynamic cities.

We have investigated the complex tapestry of the Philippines throughout this travel guidebook, revealing its historical sites, natural wonders, and distinctive customs. We have explored the depths of the Tubbataha Reefs Natural Park, gazed in astonishment at the spectacular vistas of the Chocolate Hills in Bohol, and stood in front of the exquisite Banaue Rice Terraces, which are evidence of the indigenous people's long-ago engineering prowess.

Beyond the beauty of the landscape and the wonders of the built environment, visitors are most likely to remember the people of the Philippines. The friendly welcome and sincere smiles that visitors receive are a reflection of the country's rich culture and the Bayanihan ideals, which foster a strong sense of community and group spirit. The Filipino people make every visitor feel like a member of the family, whether it's the straightforward joy of sharing a big meal with locals, taking part in a boisterous fiesta celebration, or immersing oneself in traditional arts and crafts.

It is critical to practice ethical and sustainable tourism, just like in any other travel destination. The Philippines' sensitive ecosystems and diverse wildlife necessitate that we are aware of our environmental impact. We can help ensure that this amazing country is preserved for future generations by patronizing local companies, honoring cultural norms, and protecting natural areas.

As the country sees diverse weather patterns throughout the year, be sure to take into account the optimum time to visit certain places when planning your vacation to the Philippines. Whether you're looking for the energetic nightlife of Manila, the exhilarating surf of Siargao, or the peace and quiet of remote island getaways in Palawan, the Philippines has something to offer every tourist. You may tailor your schedule to fit your hobbies, whether they be diving, hiking, bird-watching, or simply relaxing on gorgeous beaches, thanks to the abundance of islands to explore.

Do not forget to sample the regional cuisine and culture. Filipino food is a mix of flavors from cooking traditions in Spain, China, and Malaysia. Enjoy delectable foods including adobo, sinigang, lechon, and halo-halo. Engage in conversation with the people, brush up on your Tagalog language skills, and seize the chance to learn about the distinctive traditions and practices of each locale.

Last but not least, savor the tranquility and contemplation that the Philippines has to offer. The Philippines begs you to slow down, breathe, and appreciate the beauty that is all around you, whether it is by watching a mesmerizing sunset over the ocean, practicing meditation amidst the serene rice terraces, or connecting with nature in one of the many national parks.

As we say goodbye to the Philippines, we hope that our travel guidebook has given you insightful information, creative ideas, and useful advice to help you plan your own unique adventure. The Philippines is a wonderland, a patchwork of natural and cultural wonders that will captivate and amaze tourists for years to come. Pack your luggage, go out on an unforgettable vacation, and let the Philippines transform you.

Printed in Great Britain
by Amazon